KU-585-423

BEST OF

Amsterdam

Terry Carter, Lara Dunston

How to use this book

Colour-Coding & Maps

Each chapter has a colour code along the banner at the top of the page which is also used for text and symbols on maps (eg all venues reviewed in the Highlights chapter are orange on the maps). The fold-out maps inside the front and back covers are numbered from 1 to 6. All sights and venues in the text have map references; eg, (6, E2) means Map 6, grid reference E2. See p128 for map symbols.

Prices

Multiple prices listed with reviews (eg [$10/5]) usually indicate adult/concession admission to a venue. Concession prices can include senior, student, member or coupon discounts. Meal cost and room rate categories are listed at the start of the Eating and Sleeping chapters, respectively.

Text Symbols

☎   telephone

✉   address

💻   email/website address

$ admission

🕙   opening hours

ⓘ   information

♿   wheelchair access

✖   on site/nearby eatery

♟   child-friendly venue

Ⓥ   good vegetarian selection

❄   air-conditioning

✖   no-smoking rooms available

🏊   swimming pool

Best of Amsterdam
4th edition – January 2007
First published – July 2000

Published by Lonely Planet Publications Pty Ltd
ABN 36 005 607 983

Australia Head Office, Locked Bag 1, Footscray, Vic 3011
  ☎ 03 8379 8000, fax 03 8379 8111
  💻 talk2us@lonelyplanet.com.au
USA 150 Linden St, Oakland, CA 94607
  ☎ 510 893 8555, toll free 800 275 8555
  fax 510 893 8572
  💻 info@lonelyplanet.com
UK 72–82 Rosebery Ave, Clerkenwell, London
  EC1R 4RW
  ☎ 020 7841 9000, fax 020 7841 9001
  💻 go@lonelyplanet.co.uk

This title was commissioned in Lonely Planet's London office and produced by: **Commissioning Editor** Judith Bamber **Coordinating Editor** Louise Clarke **Coordinating Cartographer** Amanda Sierp **Layout Designer** Katie Thuy Bui **Editors** Justin Flynn, Emma Gilmour **Proofer** Michael Day **Cartographer** Jolyon Philcox **Managing Cartographer** Mark Griffiths **Cover Designer** Rebecca Dandens **Project Manager** Chris Love **Mapping Development** Paul Piaia **Thanks to** David Burnett, Carol Chandler, Sin Choo, Melanie Dankel, Sally Darmody, Barbara Delissen, Brendan Dempsey, Ryan Evans, Mark Germanchis, Martin Heng, Nancy Ianni, Lyahna Spencer, Gerard Walker, Celia Wood

Photographs by Lonely Planet Images and Richard Nebeský except for the following: p5, p6, p9, p10, p12, p13, p15, p16, p17, p18, p19, p20, p21, p22, p23, p25, p28, p31, p33, p34, p35, p36, p38, p50, p51, p54, p56, p57, p59, p61 (both), p71, p75, p77, p78, p82, p83, p85, p86, p87, p93, p94, p96, p97, p98, p101, p102, p105, p110 Martin Moos/Lonely Planet Images; p8 Amerens Hedwich/Lonely Planet Images; p14 Hes Mundt/Alamy; p39, p63 Carol Ann Wiley/Lonely Planet Images; p40, p41 John Elk III/Lonely Planet Images; p43 Rick Gerharter/Lonely Planet Images; p65, p70, p74, p80 Leanne Logan/Lonely Planet Images; p100 Thomas Winz/Lonely Planet Images; p107 Christian Aslund/Lonely Planet Images; p108 Juliet Coombe/Lonely Planet Images. **Cover photograph** Amsterdam café at dusk, Art Kowalsky/Photolibrary. All images are copyright of the photographers unless otherwise indicated. Many of the images in this guide are available for licensing from Lonely Planet Images: 💻 www.lonelyplanetimages.com.

ISBN 978 1 74059 971 9

Printed through Colorcraft Ltd, Hong Kong
Printed in China

Lonely Planet and the Lonely Planet logo are trademarks of Lonely Planet and are registered in the US Patent and Trademark Office and in other countries.

Lonely Planet does not allow its name or logo to be appropriated by commercial establishments, such as retailers, restaurants or hotels. Please let us know of any misuses: www.lonelyplanet.com/ip.

Although the authors and Lonely Planet have taken all reasonable care in preparing this book, we make no warranty about the accuracy or completeness of its content and, to the maximum extent permitted, disclaim all liability arising from its use.

Contents

From the Publisher

THE AUTHORS
Terry Carter

Terry left Sydney nine years ago after too long toiling in Sydney's publishing industry. Having erroneously concluded that travel writing was a far more glamorous occupation than designing books or websites, he has been travel writing for several years, mainly in Europe and the Middle East, where until recently he was based. Terry first visited Amsterdam several years ago after convincing his boss that it was 'essential' that he participate in a web conference there, and has returned frequently ever since. On this trip he had only one flat bicycle tyre. Terry has a Master's degree in media studies and divides his time between freelance travel writing and photography.

Lara Dunston

Lara has degrees in film, communications, international studies and screenwriting, and a career that before travel writing embraced writing, filmmaking and media education. Lara first visited Amsterdam for a film festival in the Spring when the sun was out and the weather warm for the first time in months, and she was struck by how many people were basking in the sun, within their homes, their curtains wide open for the world to see. She immediately fell in love with their openness, love of sunshine, and willingness to invite people into their lives. It's so *gezellig*! (See opposite)

PHOTOGRAPHER
Richard Nebeský

Richard was born one snowy night in the grungy Prague suburb of Žižkov but, surprisingly, he didn't have a camera in his hand. It was, however, not long after he got out of his cot that his father, an avid photo enthusiast, gave him his first point-and-shoot unit. Ever since, he's kept a camera by his side on treks, ski adventures, cycling trips and while researching Lonely Planet books around the globe. He has also worked for various magazines, travel guidebook publishers and on many social photography projects.

Introducing Amsterdam

Tolerance and pragmatism mixed with a spirit of *gezelligheid*. That's what makes Amsterdam so damn special. This city of 750,000 people and 600,000 bicycles is like no other in the world. Yes, it has outstanding museums, cutting-edge galleries and fantastic live music to immerse yourself in. Yes to picturesque canals that often reflect stately merchant houses in calm waters and play host to party boats where *everyone* on board is dancing to a long-forgotten '70s disco hit.

While this is all fantastic, Amsterdam's legendary tolerance and pragmatism is more so. The Dutch had the world's first homosexual marriage and Amsterdam is home to the biggest gay scene in Europe. Recognising that the world's oldest profession isn't going anywhere soon, prostitution was legalised in 1810 and brothels in 2000. The red-light district gets visited by families – try that in another capital city!

Amsterdam also realised a long time ago that a 'war on drugs' never has a clear victor and so it has the world's most tolerant drug laws. You want to get high? Go ahead. But if you think that everyone here is stoned you're wrong. Amsterdam infuriates other European capitals by having no appreciable increase in drug use despite its liberal policies.

But what really makes this offbeat capital so special? It's all about *gezellig* (pronounced heh-*zel*-ick). Amsterdammers are constantly on the lookout for it and visitors come here by the millions for it – even if they don't know what it's called when they arrive here! *Gezellig* is all about creating an environment that allows good times to happen. So what are you waiting for?

Lights on Reguliersgracht, a Southern Canal belle

Neighbourhoods

Amsterdam's charming neighbourhoods – elegantly carved by pretty waterways lined with grand canal houses – are a delight to explore.

At the city's heart is **Centrum**, only 1km long and 500m wide, but containing myriad contrasts: the atmospheric brown cafés and laid-back bars of the medieval centre, the majesty of Dam Square with its Royal Palace, the retail bustle of Kalverstraat and Nieuwendijk. In the east of Centrum you'll find the **red-light district** with its strip clubs and brothels, grungy **Nieuwmarkt** and its tourist-filled pubs and cheap restaurants, and **Waterlooplein** with its bustling market.

> **OFF THE BEATEN TRACK**
> - Laze around at Sarphatipark, where De Pijp locals relax (p33)
> - Explore the Eastern Islands and admire cutting-edge architecture (Map 4)
> - Enjoy the tranquil gardens of grand canal houses, such as the Museum Willet-Holthuysen (p24)

Waterlooplein leads to the **Plantage** with its beautiful Artis Zoo and wonderful museums. North of here is the rejuvenated **Waterfront** and the adventurous architecture of the **Eastern Islands**, such as elegant KNSM and Java, and the astonishing **IJburg**, a new residential district that is slowly rising from the sea on seven artificial islands.

Back in the centre at Muntplein, one of the Amsterdam's busiest intersections, Centrum gives way to the elegant **Southern Canal Belt** and its laid-back neighbourhoods, such as the eat street of Utrechtsestraat and the arts and antique district around Nieuwe Spiegelstraat.

Leidseplein and Rembrandtplein are the major nightlife centres – at the height of summer their squares are filled with tourists until the early hours – while nearby Reguliersdwarsstraat is home to many of Amsterdam's popular gay bars and clubs.

Southeast of Leidseplein is **Museumplein**, home to the monumental Rijksmuseum on the northeast side and the Van Gogh Museum on the southwest side. Further south is **Oud Zuid**, with its wide 19th-century boulevards and vibrant Vondelpark, an oasis of green in the middle of the city. East of here

Outside the Other Side (p97), regulars on Reguliersdwarsstraat

is multicultural **De Pijp**, with atmospheric Albert Cuypmarkt to check out by day and laid-back local restaurants and bars to explore by night.

West of Centrum you have the best part of Amsterdam, the stylish **Western Canal Belt** and characterful **Jordaan**, with their narrow lanes, such as the Nine Streets, lined with quirky specialist shops and lively cafés.

Itineraries

Amsterdam is compact and manageable on foot, so you can squeeze a lot into a day. Many attractions are within the canal belts, which take less than 45 minutes to walk across. But to get the most out of your time, rent a bicycle (see p114).

The great-value I Amsterdam Pass (see p116) gives free admission or generous discounts at most of the Highlights and scores of other museums and galleries.

> **WORST OF AMSTERDAM**
> - The open-air, male-only urinals
> - Dodging the silent killer: the bicycle
> - Bicycle theft: thousands of bikes get ripped off each year
> - Drunk and disorderly bucks-night revellers roaming the red-light district

Day One
Visit the Rijksmuseum (p21) and Van Gogh Museum (p9) before exploring the inner canals – the Singel, Herengracht, Keizersgracht and Prinsengracht. Lunch at atmospheric Café het Molenpad (p83) in the Jordaan. Check out the modern Stedelijk Museum (p14) and have sunset drinks at Eleven (p88). Wander the red-light district (p11) after dark and then eat at grand Café de Jaren (p63).

Day Two
Visit Amsterdams Historisch Museum (p15) or Anne Frank Huis (p10) before shopping the Nine Streets (p38). Lunch by the water at Spanjer en van Twist (p70) before strolling the canals to the Southern Canal Belt to explore arty Nieuwe Spiegelstraat. Dine on the eat street of Utrechtsestraat before hitting De Pijp's bars.

Day Three
Take world trip at Tropenmuseum (p16), visit Verzetsmuseum (p17) and lunch at Plancius (p76). Spend a leisurely afternoon at Artis Zoo (p22) or Vondelpark (p20). Call into the Uit Buro (p78) for concert or show tickets and taste delicious Indonesian at Blue Pepper (p66).

Tropenmuseum: hit the tropics in the heart of Amsterdam

Highlights

REMBRANDTHUIS (2, E7)

Rembrandt van Rijn (1606–69) took out a hefty mortgage to buy this 13,000 guilder house in 1639 – it was a good thing *The Night Watch* commission came along soon after.

The painter lived and worked in this grand 17th-century building for almost 20 years – until 1658 – pioneering etching techniques and painting his masterpieces. While the house was opened as a museum in 1911, it functioned more as a gallery. It wasn't until 1998 that the adjoining wing was built to house his work that Rembrandt's home was restored to look as it did in his day. His own paintings were the researchers' main source of information.

Rembrandt's light-filled painting studio is the highlight, with his easel, pigments, canvases, and shelf of armour all looking like the painter had just left them while he went down to the kitchen for a bite to eat. Another intriguing room is crammed with art objects and curiosities that Rembrandt collected – coral, seashells, dried insects, stuffed reptiles, turtle shells, animal horns, weapons, busts of Roman emperors, art books, and drawings and prints by other artists he admired – shedding light on the things that fascinated and inspired the artist.

The museum focuses as much on Rembrandt's art – particularly his etchings, of which the museum has a collection of over 250 (90% of his drawing output) – as it does on the house.

Sadly, chronic debt forced Rembrandt to move to a worker's flat at Rozengracht 184 in the Jordaan area, where he lived until his death in 1669.

THE WORLD'S FIRST GRAPHIC DESIGNER?

Design junkies and artists will find the extensive collection of Rembrandt's etchings captivating. While Rembrandt's life-size paintings, such as *The Night Watch*, receive the most attention now, during his lifetime Rembrandt's reputation was built on his tiny, intricately detailed etchings, which – because of their reproducibility – were more readily available. Rembrandt was a pioneer in the field of etching and his mastery is undisputed. Don't miss the fascinating etching room where displays of age-old etching and printing techniques take place.

VAN GOGH MUSEUM (4, B3)

The world's largest collection of work by Vincent van Gogh (1853–90) is beautifully displayed here. There are more than 200 paintings, 500 drawings, numerous sketchbooks, 570 Japanese prints belonging to Vincent and his brother Theo, and some 800 letters written by the artist – along with works by other major 19th-century artists, most of whom were friends or contemporaries, such as Toulouse-Lautrec and Paul Gauguin, or artists he admired, such as Jean-François Millet.

Arranged in chronological order and by place – for example, Antwerp 1885, Paris 1886, Arles 1888, and so on – the exhibition demonstrates the extraordinary development of Van Gogh's technique and style and the influence of his travels and environment on his art. Themed exhibits focus on specific paintings, such as *The Potato Eaters*, and things integral to his life and formation as an artist, such as *The Studio of the South*, the studio where he painted many of his masterpieces, including *Sunflowers*.

The museum also hosts superb temporary exhibitions (that have some connection to Van Gogh or the permanent collection) in a separate Kisho Kurokawa-designed wing. The 2006 Japanese Season, for example, featured three separate shows: Imperial Japan's Meiji art was complemented by Van Gogh's paintings to demonstrate his admiration for the art; *Women from Tokyo and Paris* revealed the influence of Japanese prints and paintings on leading designers; and *A Tokaido Makeover* contrasted Utagawa Hiroshige's Tokaido traditional woodcuts with Guus Rijven's contemporary photographs. Take the opportunity to see one of these multi-layered shows if you get the chance.

INFORMATION

- ☎ 570 52 00
- 🖳 www.vangoghmuseum.nl
- ✉ Paulus Potterstraat 7
- € adult/under 12yr/13-17yr €10/free/2.50
- ⏱ 10am-6pm Sat-Thu, 10am-10pm Fri
- ℹ excellent museum guides; audio tour €4
- ♿ excellent
- 🍴 museum café

THE TRAGIC LIFE OF VINCENT

Born in 1853 in Zundert, Vincent van Gogh was driven to despair by the lack of interest in his art. Beginning his training at 27, he created his best work in the last years of his life but only ever sold one painting. Suffering from severe depression, and physical and mental illness, he spent time in asylums, and in 1888 cut off part of his ear. Sadly, in 1890 he shot himself in the chest in a field near Auvers. The museum attracts over a million visitors a year, making his short life all the more tragic.

ANNE FRANK HUIS (3, B4)

Anne Frank Huis is visited by almost one million people a year, who come to see the secret rooms where young Anne wrote poignantly about her Jewish family's experience in hiding during WWII.

INFORMATION
- ☎ 556 71 05
- 🖥 www.annefrank.org
- ✉ Prinsengracht 267
- € adult/under 10yr/10-17yr €7.50/free/3.50
- 🕙 9am-9pm Mar-Sep, 9am-7pm Oct-Feb
- ℹ guide books in Museum Bookstore
- ♿ poor
- ✗ Werck (p71)

Anne's family emigrated from Frankfurt to Amsterdam in 1933. In December 1940, her father, Otto, a spice wholesaler, bought the Prinsengracht building for his business. The Germans had occupied the Netherlands six months earlier and repression of Jews had already begun. (**Amsterdams Historisch Museum** (p15) exhibits include moving testimonials describing this period.) However, it wasn't until July 1942 that Otto, his wife, 13-year-old Anne and her 16-year-old sister Margot went into hiding – with Otto's business partner, Hermann van Pels, his wife Auguste, their son Peter, and later a family friend, Fritz Pfeffer.

The families moved into the upper floors of an annexe attached to the building and lived there while their oblivious workers continued to grind spices on the floor below and the staff who helped conceal them worked next door. That was until the Nazis, on a tip, raided the building in August 1944. Anne's touching coming-of-age story, brought to life at the museum, is all the more tragic knowing that two years later she'd die in a concentration camp, her dreams of becoming a writer shattered.

The secret annexe of the house was entered by a movable bookcase concealing a stairway. Apart from this there's little left of the original furniture that filled the crammed rooms. Visitors instead rely on video testimonials, narration, captions, historical documents and their own imagination. Otto Frank wanted it this way. The only family member to survive, he published his daughter's heart-rending *Diary of Anne Frank* in 1947.

BEATING THE CROWDS
Skip the long lines by buying an Evening Ticket from the Amsterdam Tourist Offices (p120) that allows you to bypass the queues and enter the door to the left of the main entrance. Note that the queues exist because the well-managed museum carefully paces entry to ensure it's comfortable inside.

RED-LIGHT DISTRICT (2, D5)

Like any seafaring town, Amsterdam has had houses of booze and prostitution for centuries. What makes Amsterdam different (apart from the addition of the coffeeshops!) is how oddly compelling they are. While boys visiting Amsterdam for a bucks party might wonder what's not compelling about broads, booze and bud, the district also plays host to the kinds of tourists that you'd never expect to frequent such a customarily sleazy part of town.

Tour groups mingle with pimps, drug dealers and addicts, and an assortment weirdos that's second to none anywhere in the world. Bikini- and underwear-clad prostitutes, luridly neon-lit and leaning suggestively or lazily in their window boxes come in all shapes, sizes and occasionally differing percentages of being a 'complete' woman. Touts at sex theatres talk up details of what punters can expect inside, while sex shop window displays offer all sorts of oversized anatomical goodies that leave many gasping.

While Amsterdam trades to great effect on this tawdry vibe, the prostitutes here work under much better conditions than they do elsewhere. Pimps are outlawed (although they still exist), trafficking in prostitutes is illegal and the workers have a panic button they can press when they are in trouble. The red-light district is quite safe for tourists as long as you watch your bag or wallet, don't take photographs of prostitutes, or get involved with drug dealers or loiterers. For details of the area, see the walking tour on p37.

QUICK(IE) FACTS
Only 5% of the women working in the red-light district's 380-odd windows were born in the Netherlands; the majority come from the former Soviet Union and Eastern Bloc countries. Most belong to the Red Thread (the prostitutes' union), and pay around €40 to €100 per day to rent their window, depending on its location. The average cost of a quickie? From €35 to €50 is normal for 15 minutes. And the percentage of business from British clients? An 'impressive' 40%.

JORDAAN (MAP 3)

The delightful Jordaan (yoar-*darn*) – with its grand canal houses with balconies overflowing with flowers, and its lovely bridges lit up beautifully at night – is the city's most laid-back neighbourhood and ideal for exploring on foot.

INFORMATION

- ℹ VVV tourist offices (☎ 0900-400 40 40; per min €0.35)
- ♿ poor (footpaths are narrow)
- ✗ Spanjer en van Twist (p70)

Originally the working-class home of the canal-diggers, stone-masons and bridge-builders who built the Southern Canal Belt (see opposite) for Amsterdam's well-to-do during the canal-belt project of the 17th century, today it's not doing so badly itself.

Jordaan is home to some of the city's most beautiful canal house museums, a flourishing arts scene, charming specialised shops in the **Nine Streets** (p38), lively cafés, restaurants and bars, and elegant boutique hotels such as the **Hotel Pulitzer** (p100).

The name *Jordaan* is commonly thought to have come from the Bible's River Jordan or from the French *jardin* (garden), as many Huguenots (French Protestants) moved here to escape persecution in France. The area is home to many secret gardens. While the 18th century **Begijnhof** (p28) in the centre is the only one officially open to the public, there are many private gardens that once belonged to Beguines or convents just off the main streets at which you can take a discreet peek.

DON'T MISS

- Strolling the Nine Streets (p38)
- Visiting the Houseboat Museum (p23)
- Eating a canalside picnic lunch (p60)
- Admiring the grand canal houses by boat (p45)
- Chilling out at La Tertulia (p95)

By the early 1900s an average of 1000 people per hectare were living here. After WWI, new housing estates on the city's outskirts were built to relieve the pressure. Students, intellectuals, artists and professionals moved in during the 1970s, transforming Jordaan into the vibrant and dynamic neighbourhood it is today.

Drying out – Jordaan

SOUTHERN CANAL BELT (MAP 4)

Amsterdam is a city of water. Its medieval centre – itself divided by canals – is embraced by five circular waterways called the Grachtengordel or Canal Belt.

As part of the canal-belt project of the 17th century, the three main canals – Herengracht (gentlemen's canal), Keizersgracht (emperor's canal, named after Holy Roman Emperor Maximilian I) and Prinsengracht (Prince's canal, after the House of Orange) – were reserved for Amsterdam's affluent. While the rich were in positions powerful enough to ensure the authorities relaxed restrictions on the size of canalside plots, taxes were still levied according to the width of their properties, so the resourceful owners built upwards and backwards, creating a charming cityscape of tall, narrow, deep residences.

While all three canals run through the Jordaan, the part we love most is the Southern Canal Belt between Leidsestraat and the Amstel. There's much to be admired in the magnificent canal architecture, although it's the authenticity and tranquillity of the neighbourhood that makes it so lovely to explore. Take our walk (p39) or just wander.

INFORMATION
- ✉ bounded by Leidsegracht, the Singel, Singelgracht & the Amstel
- ♿ poor (footpaths are narrow)
- 🍴 Le Zinc…et Les Autres (dinner only; p75)

The Herengracht buildings are visibly grander, especially between Leidsestraat and Vijzelstraat, where the city's largest private mansions are now offices to professionals. The Keizersgracht buildings, while still impressive, are less imposing and are home to excellent museums, commercial art galleries, and antique shops. The Prinsengracht is the most charming and laid-back of all, particularly between Vijzelgracht and Utrechtsestraat – it has a down-to-earth feel, with kids playing and couples drinking wine on their front stairs in the evenings.

DON'T MISS
- Visiting the adventurous De Appel (p26) and FOAM (p26)
- Checking out the charming antique shops on Nieuwe Spiegelgracht (p46)
- Watching the local kids kick a football around at Amstelkerk
- Having a meal at a restaurant on the laid-back eat street of Utrechtsestraat

STEDELIJK MUSEUM CS (4, B3)

Amsterdam's cutting-edge contemporary art museum, the Stedelijk, or Municipal Museum, opened in 1895, the same year that the provocative Venice Biennale was born. However, the Stedelijk didn't really start to develop its own identity until the 1930s, when it was given the Van Gogh Collection by Theo van Gogh's estate. While this ended up moving next door to the purpose-built **Van Gogh Museum** (p9), it had helped establish the museum as one that was 'of the moment'.

> **INFORMATION**
> ☎ 573 29 11
> 💻 www.stedelijk.nl
> ✉ Oosterdokskade 5, Post CS Building, floors 2 & 3
> € €9/4.50
> 🕙 10am-6pm
> ⓘ 573 27 37
> ♿ good
> ✗ Eleven (p88)

Since the 1960s, the museum's focus has been on collecting contemporary art – from the avant-garde work of artists like Jean Dubuffet, Jean Tinguely and Willem de Kooning, to American Pop Art. The collection was expanded in the 1980s to include experimental video art by groundbreaking practitioners such as Bill Viola and contemporary British art by the likes of Damien Hirst and Gilbert and George. The museum also houses work of 20th century artists such as Matisse.

The Stedelijk has established a reputation for innovative arrangements of its collection, where art from different genres and moments in time are brought into juxtaposition and dialogue with one another, making for a thought-provoking and stimulating experience.

> **DON'T MISS**
> • Viewing the experimental video collection of Nam June Paik and Bill Viola
> • Dining, drinking or dancing at Eleven (p88), the funky bar on – you guessed it – the 11th floor
> • Visiting the more experimental grassroots work at Stedelijk Museum (above)

While the Museumplein headquarters next door to the Van Gogh Museum undergoes renovation (until 2009), the Stedelijk occupies two floors of the former mail-distribution office (five minutes' walk from Centraal Station).

At its temporary location, the 2nd floor displays European art and the 3rd floor exhibits post-WWII American art, showing many of the big names, such as Jackson Pollock, Piet Mondrian and Willem de Kooning.

AMSTERDAMS HISTORISCH MUSEUM (2, B6)

Amsterdam's Historical Museum provides a great introduction to the city, telling the story of its development from a small settlement on the stagnant Amstel River to a major international centre for trade in the 17th century, and to the vibrant cosmopolitan 'village' it is today.

Paintings, sculptures, scale models, ceramics and costumes, along with photographs, films, music, audio testimonials, paraphernalia from popular culture and personal keepsakes from people's lives are creatively combined to tell a complex and compelling narrative about the city and its people and their spirit of openness and tolerance.

What makes the museum really special is the everyday items, souvenirs and photos that belonged to real people, and the stories behind them. These social tales about local personalities will make you notice things you may otherwise ignore as you wander Amsterdam's streets – after reading Italian Bartolomno Rossi's story of emigrating in 1949, you'll look at Peppino's not just another Italian restaurant but as a migrant's success story.

One of the most moving exhibits focuses on footage filmed during WWII at the Alcazar Club, at 5 Thorbeckeplein, where 14 Jews had gone into hiding. Harry Saab asked a cameraman friend to document their experience once a week over several months, and the beautiful, silent black-and-white footage of people struggling to live normally is made more poignant when you learn that a May 1943 raid resulted in the arrest of 10. Harry's diary and a film script were found in 1985, so he came forward to tell his story.

INFORMATION

- ☎ 523 18 22
- 🖥 www.ahm.nl
- ✉ Nieuwezijds Voorburgwal 357
- € €6/3
- ⏱ 10am-5pm Mon-Fri, 11am-5pm Sat & Sun
- ℹ free brochure
- ♿ good
- 🍴 Luden (p64)

DON'T MISS

- Cornelius Anthoniszoon's oldest-surviving picture, *Bird's-Eye View of Amsterdam* (1538)
- A model of Sinck's Contraption (1882) used to rescue horses from the canals
- Café 't Mandje (The Basket), the city's first lesbian bar (1927)
- The 'snot-nosed' barrel organ that saved lives when Nazis fired on Dam Square crowds in 1945
- The Bijlmer exhibition – ring the door bell and get an insight into how these residents of Amsterdam's controversial housing estate lived their lives

TROPENMUSEUM (1, E4)

Visiting Amsterdam's wonderful Tropenmuseum (Museum of the Tropics) is like taking a trip around the world. A spirited celebration of global cultures, its vibrant, imaginative and interactive ethnographic exhibits cover everything from kitsch Latin American religious trinkets and captivating Day of the Dead rituals to Middle East architecture and society – featuring a life-size Yemeni house and a Cairo bazaar alley.

INFORMATION

- ☎ 568 82 15
- 🖳 www.tropenmuseum.nl
- ✉ Linnaeusstraat 2
- € adult/under 6yr/6-17yr €7.50/free/4
- 🕙 10am-5pm
- ℹ free floor plan & highlights audio tour
- ♿ good
- 🍴 museum café Ekeko

Part of the Netherlands' Royal Institute for the Tropics – a centre of intercultural collaboration that works to preserve diverse cultures, combat poverty and promote sustainable development – the enormous Tropenmuseum began life in 1910 as the Colonial Institute, which focused on colonial trade in the tropics. The Dutch role in their former colonies is honestly confronted at Tropenmuseum – an engaging exhibit on Suriname examines how the Dutch impacted on local culture, dramatically transforming it by trading in African slaves, then once slavery was abolished, importing Hindustani migrants and Javanese contract labour. The mix of African, Hindu, and Javanese-Islamic peoples resulted in a unique, vibrant society with diverse rituals, costumes and jewellery – beautifully displayed here.

Part of an absorbing exhibition on colonialism is the Cabinet of Curiosities, the fascinating displays of exotica (found in every good colonist's home) containing the obligatory dead butterflies, insects, shells, starfish, feathers and coins.

Kids love the world music exhibit – they push a button, see the instrument light up, and hear its magical sound. The museum's temporary shows also often use interactive multimedia.

DON'T MISS

- Stepping inside the life-size *yurta* (traditional felt dwelling)
- Watching the henna party video
- Taking a seat at the atmospheric Cairo bazaar café
- Admiring the wonderful puppets from around the world
- Browsing the excellent museum shop

VERZETSMUSEUM (5, B5)

The enthralling, award-winning Verzetsmuseum (Dutch Resistance Museum) tells the inspirational stories of the Dutch people who bravely resisted the Nazi occupiers from 14 May 1940 to 5 May 1945.

Through engaging exhibits incorporating official documents with personal effects and mementoes, alongside illuminated images, newsreels, films, home movies, and video and audio testimonials (in English as well as Dutch) we find out about the ways the Dutch demonstrated their resistance – from strikes, demonstrations and armed resistance, to forging documents, helping people hide and creating escape routes.

> **INFORMATION**
> ☎ 620 25 35
> 🖥 www.verzetsmuseum.org
> ✉ Plantage Kerklaan 61
> € adults/under 6yr/7-15yr
> €5.50/free/2.50
> 🕐 10am-5pm Tue-Fri, noon-5pm
> Sat-Mon
> ♿ good
> 🚊 Plancius (p76), next door

We also learn about the extraordinary, often life-threatening, dilemmas they faced and the difficult choices they made. Sometimes people just happened to be in the wrong place at the wrong time, like the manager of the tram depot who happened to take a day off to spend with his family on the day of the tram strikes – walking in the city he was caught by Nazis who believed he had coordinated the action and was avoiding arrest. They executed him to set an example.

The most personal everyday life exhibits are often the most touching – home movie footage shows a Jewish family at home, bathing a baby and mending some clothes. The next day they were deported to a processing centre, and from there to a concentration camp. Others, wearing yellow stars stitched to their clothes, carry suitcases and wave goodbye to their friends as if they are merely going away on holidays.

THE BICYCLE THIEVES

A reminder of how strongly the Netherlands still remembers German occupation during WWII is evident whenever the two countries meet at football. In the lead up to the 2006 World Cup, T-shirts bearing the slogan 'I want my bicycle back', a reference to the thousands of bicycles stolen when the Germans evacuated Amsterdam in May 1945, were big sellers. The Netherlands didn't end up playing Germany in the Cup, so the opportunity for the familiar chant 'give us back our bikes, give us back our bikes' was lost. While some still see this as harmless fun, many Amsterdammers feel that it's time to put the joke to rest.

OUDE KERK (2, D4)

The city's oldest building and earliest parish church sits incongruously in the midst of the red-light district's sea of sleaze. Initially built around 1200, the original wooden structure was replaced by a stone hall church around 1300 and consecrated in 1306. The building was subsequently extended between 1330 and 1571.

Oude Kerk was built in Dutch Brick Gothic style. Building on the muddy ground of Amsterdam required a technique still in use today – using pile-driven wooden spikes to shore up the ground before building. When expansion of the church occurred, weight was a major consideration. Inside, as you gaze at its sturdy timber beams and intricately vaulted Gothic ceiling (the largest medieval vaulted ceiling in Europe), note that these were used to limit the weight of the church (by reducing the amount of heavy bricks used).

The church is dedicated to St Nicholas, the saint of water and protector of sailors, merchants, pawnbrokers, children and prostitutes. While the people of Amsterdam hoped St Nick would protect them from the rain-swollen waters of the IJ, it wasn't water they needed protection from. In 1421 and 1452 the church miraculously survived two massive fires that engulfed the city. By 1951 the need for restoration became acute – Oude Kerk closed its doors and the work wasn't completed until 1979.

Many famous locals lie buried under the church's worn tombstones, including Rembrandt's wife, Saskia, who died in 1642 (Rembrandt himself lies in a pauper's grave in the **Westerkerk**; see p31).

INFORMATION

- ☎ 65 82 84
- 🖳 www.oudekerk.nl
- ✉ Oudekerksplein
- € €5/4
- ⏲ 11am-5pm Mon-Sat, 1-5pm Sun
- ⓘ free floor plan
- ♿ good
- ✗ Nam Kee (p64)

DON'T MISS

- Inscription above the bridal-chamber door that reads: Marry in haste, repent at leisure
- The church's stunning 1724 Müller organ
- The stained-glass windows from 1555
- The 47-bell carillon (1658) played 4.30pm on Saturdays and 2.30pm Tuesdays
- World Press Photo exhibition, held in mid-April (p27)

NEDERLANDS SCHEEPVAARTMUSEUM (5, C4)

With their long seafaring history and an obsession with water, it's only fitting that the Dutch should have such a remarkable Scheepvaartmuseum (Maritime Museum). The museum is based in the imposing Admiralty's Store building, which was designed in 1656 by Daniël Stalpaert. The East India Company (the VOC; Vereenigde Oost-Indische Compagnie) loaded their ships here before embarking on the nine-month journey to Jakarta, the VOC's Indonesian base. The admiralty vacated the building in 1973 and it has housed this collection, one of the most extensive in the world, since 1981.

> ## INFORMATION
> ☎ 523 22 22
> 💻 www.scheepvaartmuseum.nl
> ✉ Kattenburgerplein 1
> € adult//6-17yr/senior €9/4.50/7
> ⏲ 10am-5pm Tue-Sun (10am-5pm daily Jun-Aug)
> ℹ museum guidebook in English
> ♿ good
> 🍴 museum restaurant

The permanent exhibition covers the history of Dutch seafaring from the 16th century to the present. Told in chronological order, there are extensive maps, charts, globes, navigational equipment and over 500 boats – it's definitely one that lovers of all things nautical should not miss.

However, pride of place goes to the full-scale replica of the 700-tonne *Amsterdam*, moored behind the museum. This replica of one of the VOC's largest ships – keel length 42.5m – was completed in 1990 and took six years to build. The original was said to have taken six months. The original ship sank on its maiden voyage in 1748–49, taking 336 crew and passengers with it – the replica is fitted out just as it would have been for the voyage.

Another highlight is the 17m Royal Barge on display. Decorated from stem to stern in gold filigree, the barge is the oldest existing vessel in the Netherlands Navy.

SKY-HIGH

Jan Carolus Josephus van Speyk was a Dutch naval lieutenant who, rather than surrender to the Belgians after his ship was stormed near Antwerp, blew his ship (and all his crew) sky-high. While some reports say he shot a pistol into the ship's gunpowder store, the more romantic version has him throwing his lit cigar in there – perhaps having just one last puff before going up in smoke.

VONDELPARK (4, A3)

As integral a part of Amsterdam as the canals and coffeeshops, on a sunny day there's no place better than the Vondelpark. As representatives of every slice of Amsterdam's social fabric descend on this sprawling equivalent to New York City's Central Park, a party atmosphere ensues. Some kick back by reading a book, others hook up with friends and share a spliff or cradle a beer at one of the cafés, while others trade songs on beat-up guitars. Families settle in to the park's play areas, while near a fragrant rose garden, sunbathers work on their tans.

INFORMATION

- ☎ 523 77 90 (theatre & concert info); 589 14 00 (Filmmuseum)
- ▣ www.vondelpark.nl
- ✉ Stadhouderskade
- € free
- ☾ 24hr
- ♿ excellent
- ✕ Café Vertigo at the Filmmuseum (p23)

Laid out as a green belt for the Amsterdam elite's pleasure in the 1860s, the park is named after Holland's 'Shakespeare', poet and playwright Joost van den Vondel (1587–1679). The canny Amsterdammers financed the Vondelpark by reclaiming far more land than was necessary and then selling surrounding land to developers – on the condition that no factories or workers' cottages be built. Thus sprung up Oud Zuid (Old South), one of Amsterdam's most fashionable neighbourhoods.

Today the elongated park (300m by 1500m) offers a wealth of ponds, lawns, thickets and winding footpaths that encourage visitors to explore. There's almost always something happening here during summer; film buffs hit the **Filmmuseum** (see p23) where free screenings are held. Free concerts are scheduled in the open-air theatre, and the other free entertainment – musicians, mime artists, jugglers – might vary in quality, but add to the fantastic atmosphere.

BETTER LONG-HAIRED THAN SHORT-SIGHTED

In 1967 word spread that Amsterdam had tuned in and turned on, so hordes of hippies descended on the Vondelpark to drop out. The park became famous worldwide as an open-air dormitory with copious amounts of soft drugs and free love, supported by the catch-cry 'Better Long-Haired than Short-Sighted'. As the idealism softened and the drugs hardened, the scene dissipated, but you'll still see a few '60s hippy types in the park – and some of them can even remember the Summer of Love…

RIJKSMUSEUM (4, C3)

The monumental Rijksmuseum, the 'Louvre' of Amsterdam, is the Netherlands' largest and most important museum, with a collection of more than a million objects of art, including 5000 paintings, dating from 1400 to 1900.

The very finest of its Dutch collection, The Masterpieces, in the Philips Wing, is all that's on show until 2008 while the main building undergoes renovation.

The Rijksmuseum opened its doors in 1800 in The Hague's Huis ten Bosch (residence of Queen Beatrix). King Louis Bonaparte moved the museum to Amsterdam in 1808 and added Rembrandt's *The Night Watch* to its impressive collection. In 1885 the Rijksmuseum was moved to the monumental Pierre Cuypers-designed building in Museumplein, the museum district.

INFORMATION
- ☎ 674 70 47 (24 hr)
- 🖥 www.rijksmuseum.nl
- ✉ Jan Luijkenstraat 1
- € adult/under 18yr €10/free
- 🕐 9am-6pm Sat-Thu, 9am-10pm Fri
- ℹ free floor plan; audio tour €4
- ♿ excellent
- ✗ Patou (p73)

The Netherlands was one of the richest countries in the world in the 17th century, known as The Golden Age, and The Masterpieces well illustrates this period of prosperity and power in which the arts flourished. Representing one-eighth of the museum's total collection, the exhibition is organised by theme and includes the most popular works: Rembrandt's dramatic *The Night Watch*, Vermeer's *Kitchen Maid* and Frans Hals' *The Merry Drinker*. Begin in the Dutch Republic room, where you'll have to battle with disoriented crowds on your way to the World Power exhibit – don't miss Hendrik van Schuylenburg's splendid *VOC Base at Hougly in Bengal* (1665). Next, fascinating rooms display intricate dolls' houses, riches of the Treasury, and collections of beautiful blue-and-white delftware. Upstairs are rooms devoted to the wonderful work of Frans Hals, Rembrandt and his pupils, and Johannes Vermeer.

DON'T MISS
- Hendrick Avercamp's chilly *Winter Landscape with Ice Skaters* (1609)
- Johannes Vermeer's delightful Delft scene, *The Little Street* (1658)
- Pieter de Hooch's touching *A Mother's Duty* (1658)
- Jan Davidsz de Heem's luxuriant *Festoon of Fruits and Flowers* (1660)
- Petronella Oortman's intricate miniature doll's house that cost the price of a canal house!

ARTIS ZOO (5, C6)

The world's third-oldest zoo (and the oldest in mainland Europe) is the place to bring children in Amsterdam. Located right in the heart of a busy neighbourhood and laid out in the former Plantage gardens, locals as well as tourists visit to stroll its lush, well-manicured paths.

INFORMATION

- ☎ 523 34 00
- 🖥 www.artis.nl
- ✉ Plantage Kerklaan 38-40
- € adult/3-9yr/senior €16/12.50/15
- 🕑 9am-6pm (5pm in winter)
- ℹ layout maps
- ♿ excellent
- ✄ in the zoo, or at Plancius (p76), nearby

The zoo was founded in 1838 by an association called Natura Artis Magistra (Latin for 'Nature is the Master of Art') who aimed to link nature and art. Packed with listed 19th-century buildings and monuments, it feels like a zoological museum. Today it features around 700 species of animals and 200 different species of trees. From January to May, when the flowers bloom, it's a riot of colour.

In addition to the expected zoo attractions – the big cats, apes and gorillas – the African savannah is a highlight. Alongside zebras and other African species, you'll spot the scimitar-horned oryx – once found in the Sahara and virtually extinct in the wild – now part of a successful breeding programme.

The aquarium is another highlight. Built in 1882 and renovated in the late 1990s, the graceful purpose-built hall has almost 2000 fish. The tanks are enormous and the variety of colourful fish, stunning. The must-see exhibit here is the tank featuring a cross-section of an Amsterdam canal, complete with sad sunken bicycles and eels.

DON'T MISS
- The zoo's indoor rainforest
- Daily feedings – check times as you enter
- The children's playground
- The Planetarium

There is also a children's farm where kids can pet goats, calves and other cuddly critters – don't miss the cute local tufted ducks!

Practise your Parsel Tongue at Artis Zoo

Sights & Activities

MUSEUMS

Allard Pierson Museum (2, C7)

The University of Amsterdam's engaging archaeological museum exhibits ancient Egyptian, Greek, Roman and Near East artefacts dating from 4000 BC to AD 500 as well as scale models of temples and monuments. There's a fascinating room dedicated to mummies.

☎ 525 25 56 🖳 www .cf.uba.uva.nl/apm ✉ Oude Turfmarkt 127 € €5/2.50 🕑 10am-5pm Tue-Fri, 1-5pm Sat & Sun 🕭 good

Bijbels Museum (2, A7)

Housed in two stately canalside buildings, the Biblical Museum takes you on a journey through the stories of the Bible via models of temples, the Tabernacle, biblical scenes, Egyptian antiquities, archaeological finds and a collection of rare Bibles.

☎ 624 24 36 🖳 www .bijbelsmuseum.nl ✉ Herengracht 366-368 € €6/3, plus €1.50 surcharge special exhibitions 🕑 10am-5pm Mon-Sat, 11am-5pm Sun 🕭 fair

EnergeticA (5, D6)

This stunning museum in an atmospheric former power station has dynamic exhibits on energy, the invention of electrical appliances and the development of technology, along with some wonderful antique electrics on display.

☎ 422 12 27 🖳 www .energetica.nl in Dutch ✉ Hoogte Kadijk 400 € €4 🕑 10am-4pm Mon-Fri 🕭 good

Filmmuseum (4, A2)

Along with the largest film library in the Netherlands and a wonderful screening programme at two venues (p90), the Filmmuseum has an excellent information centre in a building on Vondelstraat

69-71 with 1900 journals, 30,000 books, screenplays, biographies, CD-Roms, DVDs, clippings and posters.

☎ 589 14 00 🖳 www .filmmuseum.nl ✉ Vondelpark 3 🕑 9am-10.15pm € €2.50-11 🕭 good

Hollandsche Schouwburg (5, B5)

Built in 1892 in the Jewish quarter, the Dutch Theatre was renamed the Jewish Theatre by the Nazis in 1941, then used as a Jewish deportation centre from 1942 to 1943. Thousands were sent to death camps, resulting in the extermination of 104,000 Dutch Jews. A memorial and exhibition describes this period.

☎ 531 03 40 🖳 www .hollandscheschouwburg.nl ✉ Plantage Middenlaan 24 🕑 11am-4pm 🕭 good

Houseboat Museum (3, B5)

If you're curious to learn how people lived on *woonboot* (houseboats), then check out the *Hendrika Maria*, a former commercial sailing ship, built in 1914. They're probably more spacious than you'd envisaged, however the toilets probably smell worse than you imagined.

☎ 427 07 50 🖳 www .houseboatmuseum.nl ✉ opposite Prinsengracht 296 € €3/2.25 🕑 11am-5pm Tue-Sun Mar-Oct, 11am-5pm Fri-Sun Nov-Feb, closed Jan

Joods Historisch Museum (2, F8)

The enormous Great Synagogue, dating from 1675, is

Navel gazing at Museum Amstelkring (p24)

home to two exhibitions – the History of the Jews in the Netherlands 1600–1890, and Religion, about Judaism and Jewish traditions. The museum also organises walking tours of the Jewish quarter. ☎ 531 03 10 💻 www.jhm.nl ✉ Nieuwe Amstelstraat 1 € €6.50/3 ☉ 11am-5pm ♿ excellent

Multatuli Museum (2, B2)
This small but fascinating museum-home gives an insight into the life of Dutch East Indies novelist Multatuli (meaning 'I have suffered greatly' in Latin), pseudonym of Eduard Douwes Dekker (1820–87), best known for shedding light on race relations in his work *Max Havelaar* (1860). ☎ 638 19 38 💻 www.multatuli-museum.nl ✉ Korsjespoortsteeg 20 ☉ 10am-5pm Tue, noon-5pm Sat & Sun, closed Sat in July & Aug

Museum Amstelkring (2, E4)
Secreted away in this grand canal house is 'Our Lord in the Attic', a former clandestine church, built in 1661 when Catholicism was officially banned by the Calvinists. The elegant living, kitchen and chaplain's room give an intriguing insight into 17th-century domestic life. ☎ 624 66 04 💻 www.museumamstelkring.nl ✉ Oudezijds Voorburgwal 40 € €7/5 ☉ 10am-5pm Mon-Sat, 1-5pm Sun

Museum Van Loon (4, D2)
Willem van Loon, a cofounder of the Dutch East India Company, was one of Amster-dam's wealthiest and most powerful men. His ancestors' opulent home with its sumptuous Louis XV furnishings is evidence of the Van Loons' affluence and nobility. ☎ 624 52 55 💻 www.museumvanloon.nl ✉ Keizersgracht 672 € €6/4 ☉ 11am-5pm Fri-Mon Sep-Jun, daily Jul-Aug ♿ poor

Museum Willet-Holthuysen (2, D8)
Abraham Willet liked expensive things, so it was a good thing he married a wealthy woman. Louisa Holthuysen generously bequeathed the City their magnificent mansion and the collection of treasures her husband amassed – furniture, paintings, ceramics, silver, glasswork and even photographs purchased on the couple's extensive late-19th-century travels. ☎ 523 18 22 💻 www.willetholthuysen.nl ✉ Herengracht 605 € €4/2 ☉ 10am-5pm Mon-Fri, 11am-5pm Sat & Sun ♿ fair

Nationaal Vakbondsmuseum (5, A5)
While you'll learn something about Dutch trade unions in what was once the home of the General Netherlands Diamond Workers Union, another reason to visit is to admire the monumental building. Designed by HP Berlage, the museum is Mediterranean in feel. It has yellow, blue and white glazed brick, a magnificent lamp hanging from the cupola, and a stunning staircase. ☎ 624 11 66 💻 www.deburcht-vakbondsmuseum.nl ✉ Henri Polaklaan 9 € €2.50/1.25 ☉ 11am-5pm Mon-Fri, 1-5pm Sun ♿ fair

NEMO (5, B3)
Resembling an enormous moss-covered sinking ship, Renzo Piano's stunning edifice is home to an excellent interactive science and technology museum with hands-on laboratories, engaging exhibits and superb city views from the rooftop. ☎ 531 32 33 💻 www.e-nemo.nl ✉ Oosterdok 2 € adult/under 4yr €11.50/free ☉ 10am-5pm Tue-Sun Sep-Jun, daily Jul-Aug ♿ good

Pianola Museum (3, B3)
One for pianola fans only, the emphasis here (in probably Amsterdam's smallest

Interactive science, sure, but will they find NEMO?

THE DEMISE OF JEWISH AMSTERDAM

When the Jews were expelled from Spain and Portugal in the 1500s, many found Amsterdam a safe place to live and practise their religion. By 1941 most Jews in the Netherlands were living in Amsterdam and the Jewish population was around 80,000. By Liberation in May 1945, it was 5000. It's hard to determine if non-Jewish Amsterdam knew what was happening, because the Germans systematically uprooted, marginalised and isolated the Jewish community in a way that made its fate unclear to the rest of the populace. The Joods Historisch Museum (Jewish Historical Museum; p23) is a great place to find out more.

museum) is on the delicate perforated paper music rolls – nearly 20,000 of them – rather than the 20-odd pianolas on display.
☎ 627 96 24 🖳 www .pianola.nl ✉ Westerstraat 106 💶 €5/3/4 🕑 2-5pm Sun 🕭 good

Press Museum (1, F3)
Media practitioners will appreciate this small Press Museum, the national repository for the Netherlands' journalistic heritage. Its extensive collection of newspapers, illustrated magazines, posters, publicity materials, original political drawings, photographs and documents are organised into two to three engaging exhibitions a year.
☎ 692 88 10 🖳 www .persmuseum.nl
✉ Zeeburgerkade 10
💶 €3.50/2.50 🕑 10am-5pm Tue-Fri, noon-5pm Sun 🕭 fair

Theatermuseum (2, A4)
This majestic canal house museum of Dutch theatre is a must for theatre lovers, for its extravagant costumes, intricate set models, and fascinat-

ing posters and photos. Built in 1638 by famous architect Hedrik de Keyser, the splendid interior is richly decorated, the highlight of which is a dramatic spiral staircase.
☎ 551 33 00 ✉ Herengracht 168 💶 €4.50/2.25 🕑 11am-5pm Mon-Fri, 1-5pm Sat & Sun 🕭 fair

Tram Museum (1, B4)
This museum in motion allows tram lovers to take a one-hour trip back in time, from the historic 1916 Haarlemmermeer Station through the beautiful Amsterdamse Bos (p32), on a lovely old tram from the Tram Museum's wonderful collection.

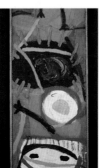

Kind, Zon en Vogel, Karel Appel (1950), CoBrA Museum

Tours run approximately every 30 minutes.
☎ 673 75 38 Sundays only 🖳 www.museumtram.nl
✉ Haarlemmermeer Station, Amstelveenseweg 264
💶 €3.50/1.80 🕑 11am-5pm Sun, Easter Sunday-Oct, 11am-5pm Wed & Sun, Jul & Aug 🚍 16 🕭 fair

GALLERIES

Commercial art galleries open and close all the time in Amsterdam, so for up-to-date gallery listings check out Exhibitions Amsterdam available online at www.akka.nl. The Spui plays host every weekend from March through to December (10am–6pm) to an open-air art market, Art on Sundays Amsterdam, featuring the work of around 60 artists on rotation. More information is available online at www .artplein-spui.nl.

ARCAM (4, B4)
Located in a stunningly shaped building (p27), Amsterdam's Centre for Architecture (ARCAM) should be the first point of call for architecture and urban design buffs. Staff can suggest buildings to see to match your interests, while ARCAM has regular exhibitions on Dutch and international architecture.
☎ 620 48 78 🖳 www .arcam.nl ✉ Prins Hendrikkade 600 🕑 1-5pm Tue-Sat 🕭 good

CoBrA Museum (1, B6)
CoBrA stands for Copenhagen Brussels Amsterdam,

where CoBrA movement artists Asger Jorn, Joseph Noiret, Christian Dotremont, Constant Corneille and Karel Appel came from. Cosignatories to 1948 manifesto 'The Case Was Heard' (in opposition to the Surrealists' 'The Case Is Heard'), their primitive style rejuvenated Flemish art. Their influential work is exhibited here.

☎ 547 50 50 🖳 www .cobra-museum.nl ✉ Sandbergplein 1 € adults/child 6-16yr, seniors/students €7/3/4 ☾ 11am-5pm Tue-Sun ♿ good

De Appel (4, D1)

This cutting-edge contemporary art space holds adventurous but accessible exhibitions of conceptual art – including photography, painting, film, multimedia and mixed media installations – grounded in theory but making connections with everyday life.

☎ 622 56 51 🖳 www .deappel.nl ✉ Nieuwe Spiegelstraat 10 € €4/2 ☾ 11am-6pm Tue-Sun ♿ excellent

Felix Meritis (3, B5)

Founded in 1777 to promote the arts and sciences, today Felix Meritis' mission is to connect cultures. This dynamic multidisciplinary arts and intellectual space holds stimulating photographic, art and new media exhibitions; symposiums, lectures and debates; and musical performances and events.

☎ 626 23 21 🖳 www.felix .meritis.nl ✉ Keizersgracht 324 ☾ 9am-end of event ♿ fair

FOAM (4, D2)

One for photography enthusiasts, the small Fotografiemuseum Amsterdam (FOAM) shows stimulating and challenging exhibitions in all photographic genres. Exhibitions change every couple of months. The centre also plays a role in developing local talent by providing a space for collaboration between photographers.

☎ 551 65 00 🖳 www .foam.nl ✉ Keizersgracht 609 € €6.50/5 ☾ 10am-5pm Sat-Wed, 10am-9pm Thu & Fri ♿ fair

Galerie Fons Welters (3, A4)

Fons Welters has been actively involved in identifying, nurturing and representing local talent since establishing the contemporary art gallery in 1988. A small project space at the front of the gallery, Playstation, showcases the work of emerging artists.

☎ 423 30 46 ✉ Bloemstraat 140 ☾ 1-6pm Tue-Sat ♿ good

Hermitage Amsterdam (4, F1)

This satellite of the Hermitage Museum in St Petersberg shows splendid exhibitions from the Russian collection, that have so far included an

impressive display of objects of art belonging to Tsar Nicholas and Tsarina Alexandra and stunning filigree collected by Catherine the Great and Peter the Great.

☎ 530 87 51 🖳 www .hermitage.nl ✉ Nieuwe Herengracht 14 € 7/free ☾ 10am-5pm ♿ good

Huis Marseille (3, C6)

This private canal house museum holds eclectic exhibitions of international contemporary photography in its five spacious rooms and lovely summerhouse in the garden. It also shows independent films, holds discussion evenings, and there is a terrific little library and 'Media Kitchen' where you can watch experimental videos.

☎ 531 89 89 🖳 www .huismarseille.nl ✉ Keizersgracht 401 € 5/3 ☾ 11am-5pm Tue-Sun

Nieuwe Kerk (2, B4)

Finished in 1408, the New Church is 'new' compared to the Old Church (Oude Kerk; p18). When not hosting coronations (Queen Beatrix, 1980) and royal weddings (Prince of Orange to Princess Maxima, 2002), it's host to wonderful exhibitions of treasures from other cultures and countries.

AMSTERDAM FOR FREE

- Join the in-line skaters outside the Filmmuseum (p23; 8pm Friday) for a 15km skate through the city
- Admire the art galleries and historical canal houses in the Jordaan
- Wander through the Amsterdams Historisch Museum's free Civic Guard Gallery (p15)
- Wander through the Vondelpark (p20) – there's always *something* interesting going on!

☎ 638 69 09 ⌨ www
.nieuwekerk.nl ✉ Dam
Square € €4 ☉ 10am-
6pm & good

Netherlands Media Art Institute (3, C5)

Also known as Montevideo/
Time Based Arts, this cutting-
edge space holds provocative
new-media exhibitions,
installations, performances
and film screenings, as well
as supporting research,
reflection, distribution and
promotion of new technolo-
gies in the media arts.
☎ 623 71 01 ⌨ www
.montevideo.nl ✉ Keiz-
ergracht 264 € €2.50/1.50
☉ Gallery 1-6pm Tue-Sat,
Mediatheque 1-5pm Mon-Fri
& good

Reflex Modern Art Gallery (4, C2)

Reflex's Modern and (across
the road) New Art Gallery
(see below) are two of
Amsterdam's best commer-
cial galleries, showing work
by important artists such
as Karel Appel, Asger Jorn,
Willem de Kooning, Joseph
Beuys, Jeff Koons, Christo
and even Pablo Picasso.
☎ 627 28 32 ⌨ www
.reflex-art.nl ✉ Watering-
schans 79A ☉ 11am-6pm
Tue-Sat & good

Reflex New Art Gallery (4, C2)

The Reflex New Art Gallery
tends to be more adventurous than its older sibling,
representing less mainstream
painters and photographers
such as Roger Ballen, David
LaChapelle, Erwin Olaf, Chris
Verene, Bill Owens and Nobuy-
oshi Araki, to name a few.
☎ 627 28 32 ⌨ www
.reflex-art.nl ✉ Watering-
schans 83 ☉ 11am-6pm
Tue-Sat & good

Stedelijk Museum Bureau Amsterdam (3, B5)

The Stedelijk Museum's
contemporary project art
space is situated in a former
clothing warehouse in an
arty neighbourhood. Its focus
is on adventurous new trends
in installation, photography,
painting, sculpture, design
and new media, so its work
tends to be more experimental in approach.
☎ 422 04 71 ⌨ www
.smba.nl ✉ Rozenstraat
59 ☉ 11am-5pm Tue-Sun
& poor

World Press Photo, Oude Kerk (2, D4)

World Press Photo, the largest annual international
photojournalism competition
(in 2006, 4448 photog-
raphers entered 83,044
photos!) is shown for two
months at the Oude Kerk and
is not to be missed. Judged
in Amsterdam, the extraordinary 200 prize-winning
photos show here before
touring 85 cities worldwide.
☎ 676 60 96 ⌨ www
.worldpressphoto.nl
✉ Oudekerksplein 23
€ €5/4 ☉ 11am-5pm
Mon-Sat, 1-5pm Sun
& good

NOTABLE BUILDINGS & MONUMENTS

ARCAM (4, B4)

Built on foundations of a
pavilion designed by Renzo
Piano, this fascinating
structure, completed in 2003,
is a fitting home for Amsterdam's Centre for Architecture
(ARCAM). Wrapping a zinc-
coated corrugated aluminium

Nieuwe Kerk's divine interior

NARROW-MINDED

Property in Amsterdam was once taxed on frontage – the narrower the house, the lower the tax. Hence there are a few extremely slim specimens around town. Two of the narrowest to look out for are Oude Hoogstraat 22, east of Dam Square (2, D6), only 2.02m wide and 6m deep; and Singel 166 (2, B3), a mere 1.8m across the front, but widening to a generous 5m at the rear.

skin around an irregular-shaped shell, architect René van Zuuk has managed to give each façade a different feel.
☎ 620 48 78 ⬚ www .arcam.nl ✉ Prins Hendrikkade 600 ◷ 1-5pm Tue-Sat ♿ good

Bartolotti House (2, A4)
Next door to the Theatermuseum (p25), this lovely private residence, built in 1615 by Hendrick de Keyser (1565–1621), has one of Amsterdam's most stunning façades: a red-brick Dutch Renaissance classic that follows the bend in the canal and has wonderful detail. Not open to the public.
✉ Herengracht 170-172 ♿ good

Begijnhof (2, B7)
This secluded Begijnhof, one of many *hofjes* (little courtyards) in Amsterdam, was home to the Beguines, a Catholic sisterhood of chaste unwed women from wealthy families. Dating from the early 14th century, it consists of tiny gabled houses grouped around tranquil, well-kept courtyards. The last community member died in 1971.
☎ 622 19 18 ✉ Spui, north side ⬚ www .begijnhofamsterdam.nl ◷ 8am-5pm ♿ excellent

Beurs van Berlage (2, D4)
Named after Dutch master architect Hendrik Petrus

(HP) Berlage (1856–1934), this former stock exchange (1903) is one of Amsterdam's most striking buildings, with strong, clean lines and a powerful presence. This was Berlage's first major commission and today he is considered the father of modern architecture in the Netherlands.
✉ Damrak 277 ⬚ www .bvb.nl ♿ good

Centraal Station (2, E2)
Built in Dutch Renaissance revival style (1882–89) with Gothic revival elements, the architects of this edifice were Pierre Cuypers (who also designed the Rijksmuseum, p21) and AL van Gendt, the architect of the Concertgebouw (right).
✉ Stationsplein 51 ♿ excellent

Concertgebouw (4, B4)
One of the most heavily commissioned architects of his time, AL van Gendt designed this neo-Renaissance classic (1888), one of the most popular concert halls in the world. While the building was listed in 1972, the controversial (read: unconditionally ugly) glass foyer was added in 1988.
☎ 675 44 11 ⬚ www .concertgebouw.nl ✉ Concertgebouwplein 2-6 ♿ excellent

Dam Square & Nationaal Monument (2, C5)
This pigeon- and performance artist-filled expanse was the site of the original dam built across the Amstel, giving the city its name. Filled in 1672, it became the central market square. The obelisk at its eastern end is

Damned bright in Dam Square on Queen's Day

the Nationaal Monument, built in 1956 to honour the fallen in WWII.
⊠ Dam Square ♿ excellent

De Burcht (5, B5)
The Trade Union Museum, former home of the powerful General Netherlands Diamond Workers' Union, was designed by architect HP Berlage in 1900. Its muscular look gives it the appearance of a castle.
☎ 624 11 66 ⌨ www.deburcht-vakbondsmuseum.nl ⊠ Henri Polaklaan 9 € €3/2 ⏰ 11am-5pm Tue-Fri ♿ fair

De Gooyer Windmill (5, E6)
This former grain mill dating from 1814 is the sole survivor of five windmills that once stood in this part of town. In 1985 the former public baths alongside were converted into a small brewery, the Bierbrouwerij 't IJ (p87), that is perfect for a tipple. Tours 4pm Friday.
☎ 622 83 25 ⊠ Funenkade 7 ⏰ 3-7.45pm Wed-Sun (brewery) ♿ fair

De Waag (2, E5)
The oldest secular public building in Amsterdam (1488), the Weigh House was originally one of the gates in the city wall. Rebuilt as a weigh station in the 17th century, it later served as a guildhouse, a courthouse and place of execution. Today it accommodates a café-restaurant.
☎ 422 77 72 ⊠ Nieuwmarkt square ♿ excellent

Engelse Kerk (2, B7)
The prim little Gothic English Reformed Church

The Greenpeace Building: Art Deco, yes; green, no

in the Begijnhof (p28) was built around 1400 and was originally Catholic, but today serves as the city's Presbyterian church, ministering mainly to British and Scottish expats. Its excellent acoustics lure lots of classical ensembles using period instruments.
☎ 624 96 65 (concert ticket info) ⊠ Begijnhof 48 ♿ fair

Greenpeace Building (3, C4)
This former insurance office, built in 1904–05 by Gerrit van Arkel, is a rare example of Nieuwe Kunst (Dutch Art Nouveau) architecture in Amsterdam. It's still known as the 'Greenpeace Building', though they moved long ago.
⊠ Keizersgracht 174-176 ♿ good

Het Schip (1, C2)
The highlight of the fascinating Spaarndammer area is Het Schip (The Ship), a massive workers' apartment building. Designed by Michel de Klerk, it was completed in 1920 and is a classic of the Amsterdam School architectural movement of the early 20th century. The museum offers fascinating insights into the architecture.

☎ 418 28 85 ⌨ www.hetschip.nl ⊠ Spaarndammerplantsoen 140 € adult/child/concession €5/2/2.75 ⏰ 1-5pm Wed-Sun ⊠ Spaarndammerstraat & Zaanstraat

House on the Three Canals (2, C6)
This charming 1609–10 Dutch Renaissance house located on a pretty spot across from the university was previously owned by a succession of prominent Amsterdam families.
⊠ Oudezijds Achterburgwal 249 ♿ excellent

House with the Heads (2, A3)
This Dutch Renaissance classic (1622) is notable for its richly decorated façade as well the six heads (at door level) representing the classical deities. Folklore has it that the heads are actually of burglars decapitated by an axe-wielding maid of the original owner!
⊠ Keizersgracht 123 ♿ excellent

IJburg Bridges (1, F4)
The first of several bridges linking the IJburg (p30) to

IJBURG (1, F4)

The IJburg is being developed to help solve Amsterdam's housing problems. The plan, creating seven new islands on IJmeer, Amsterdam's lake, goes back as far back as 1965. While the city council finally gave the go-ahead in 1996, a series of objections saw the project go to a referendum in 1997. While a huge majority voted against the islands being built, not enough Amsterdammers voted, so the project got the nod. The first building on the islands was opened in 2001 and when it is finished in 2012, the seven isles will have 45,000 new residents living in around 18,000 new homes.

the mainland, the initial bridge, has an engaging, curvaceous, wave-shaped profile and two separate decks. This being Amsterdam, its silhouette has been compared to a pair of breasts more than once…
⊠ IJburg ♿ excellent

Koninklijk Paleis (2, B5)

The Royal Palace was commissioned as a town hall in 1648, completed in 1662, and became a royal palace in 1808. Designed by Jacob van Campen, its sombre façade belies a lavish interior that is unfortunately closed to visitors until at least 2009.
⊠ Dam Square 🖥 www.koninklijkhuis.nl
♿ excellent

Magere Brug (3, F2)

While the name translates to 'Skinny Bridge', the name of this romantic and much-photographed (especially at night) bridge is often attributed to the Mager sisters, who built a narrow footbridge here in the 17th century. Clearly no longer skinny, the narrow bridge was later replaced.
⊠ Kerkstraat on the River Amstel ♿ good

Magna Plaza (2, B4)

Amsterdam's former main post office, Magna Plaza was built between 1899 and 1908 in a portentous neo-Gothic and neo-Renaissance style. With domes, turrets and gargoyles, it's more suggestive of a fairytale castle than a post office. Today, despite the myriad clothing boutiques inside, it's still worth a peek.
⊠ Nieuwezijds Voorburgwal 182 🖥 www.magnaplaza.nl
♿ excellent

Noorderkerk (2, A1)

This Calvinist church (1632) is notable for the drastic departure in design for architects Hendrik de Keyser and Hendrik Jacobszoon Staets. Built in the shape of a broad Greek cross (four arms of equal length) around a central pulpit, it's one of the first of its kind in the Netherlands.
☎ 624 78 19 🖥 www.noorderkerkconcerten.nl (for concerts, in Dutch)
⊠ Noordermarkt
♿ excellent

No petty affair: the Chamber of Commissions for Petty Affairs at Koninklijk Paleis

Oostindisch Huis (2, D6)
This impressive, muscular building is the former headquarters of the mighty VOC (Vereenigde Oost-Indische Compagnie), the United East India Company. The building was completed in 1605 (three years after the company formed) and the façade has remained relatively intact. It's now part of Amsterdam University.
✉ Kloveniersburgwal, cnr Oude Hoogstraat ♿ excellent

Portuguese-Israelite Synagogue (2, F7)
Europe's largest synagogue when it was built by the Sephardic community between 1671 and 1675, this building still stays true to the original intent despite several restorations. While architecturally inspired by the Temple of Solomon in Jerusalem, the building's classical lines are not as interesting as the synagogue's remarkable interior.
☎ 624 53 51 ⌨ www .esnoga.com ✉ Mr Visserplein 3 € €6.50/5 ⏰ 10am-4pm Sun-Fri Apr-Oct, 10am-4pm Sun-Thu, 10am-4pm Sun-Thu, 10am-3pm Fri Sep-Mar ♿ good

Stopera (2, E7)
Officially called the Stadhuis-Opera, this charmless, chunky white city-hall-cum-opera (completed in 1986) is still known as 'Stopera' for the protests that delayed its construction for nearly two decades.
☎ 625 54 55 ⌨ www .hetmuziektheater.nl ✉ Waterlooplein 22 ♿ good

Stop and admire the lights of the 'Stopera'

Trippenhuis (2, E6)
Making their fortune arms dealing, the Trip brothers commissioned young Dutch architect Justus Vingboons to build the Trippenhuis in 1660. It's a grey-stone mansion with eight Corinthian pilasters across two houses (one for each brother) and in a nod to their profession, the chimneys are shaped like mortars. Not open to the public.
✉ Kloveniersburgwal 29 ♿ good

Tropenmuseum (1, E4)
In 1913 JJ van Nieukerken was chosen as the architect of this captivating museum (p16), however death in the same year saw his son, MA van Nieukerken take over. Further problems – arguments over the style, costs, scarcity of materials due to the war – delayed its opening until 1926.
☎ 568 82 15 ⌨ www .tropenmuseum.nl ✉ Linnaeusstraat 2 € adult/under 6yr/6-17yr €7.50/free/4 ⏰ 10am-5pm ♿ good

Tuschinskitheater (2, C8)
Built in 1921, this handsome theatre intermingles Art Deco and Amsterdam School architecture. Faithfully restored, the interior features a huge handmade

carpet and a striking cupola that should never meet the gaze of someone taking hallucinogens. Sadly, you'll have to endure a Hollywood blockbuster to eyeball the marvellous interior.
☎ 626 26 33 ⌨ www .pathe.nl in Dutch ✉ Reguliersbreestraat 26 ⏰ noon-10pm ♿ excellent

Vondelkerk (4, A2)
Architect Pierre Cuypers' favourite church (1870–80), it suffered from lack of funds during construction and a fire in 1904, and was marked for demolition in 1978. It's an attractive church, featuring a fascinating series of shapes, with an octagon as its base.
✉ Vondelstraat 77 ⏰ 8am-6pm ♿ good

Westerkerk (3, B4)
The Westerkerk was the world's largest Protestant church when completed in 1631. Designer Hendrick de Keyser (1565–1621), who designed the Zuiderkerk (p32) and Bartolotti House (p28), died soon after construction began. His son Pieter completed it. Rembrandt lies here in a pauper's grave. Climbing the 85m-high tower is sometimes possible.
☎ 624 77 66 ⌨ www.westerkerk.nl

✉ Prinsengracht 279-281
€ free; tower €5
🕐 church 11am-3pm
Mon-Sat Apr-Sep, tower
10am-5pm Mon-Sat Apr-Sep
♿ church good, tower none

Zuiderkerk (2, E6)
Amsterdam's first commissioned Protestant church (1602–11) was based on a Catholic design but without the choir. Today it's primarily a planning and public-housing information centre with audiovisual exhibits. The interior has been modernised and you may be able to climb the tower between June and September for a great view.
☎ 622 29 62 ✉ Zuiderkerkhof 72 🕐 9am-4pm Mon-Fri, noon-4pm Sat
♿ fair (tower, none)

PARKS & GARDENS

Amsterdam is a leafy city, with plenty of shady trees by the canals where people smoke funny-smelling cigarettes. And while Vondelpark (p20) is the oasis of choice for most tired urbanites, there are scores of smaller parks and gardens where you can soak up the rays. In spring, these beautiful places burst with tulips, hyacinths and daffodils.

Kids amusing themselves at Museumplein

Amstelpark (1, D6)
This rambling green space in southwest Amsterdam is notable for its redolent rose garden and rhododendron walk. Outside the southern end is a sparkling example of an Amsterdam windmill (the De Rieker, which cranks up only on the second Saturday in May, National Windmill Day).
✉ Europaboulevard
🕐 dawn-dusk ♿ excellent

Amsterdamse Bos (1, B6)
The city's largest recreational area, on weekends nature-loving locals flock to the Bos (forest) to enjoy its lakes and meadows. Laid out in the 1930s, it's 20 times larger than Vondelpark – and feels 100 times less crowded! Take buses 170, 171, 172 or tram 5.
☎ 643 14 14
✉ Koenenkade 56 🕐 24hr
♿ excellent

Hortus Botanicus (5, A5)
This delightful botanical garden, one of the world's oldest, opened in 1682. Originally a medicinal herb garden (1638), it expanded during the 17th and 18th centuries with the Dutch empire. Today the gardens and greenhouses hold more than 4000 plant species, and the world's oldest potted plant, a 300-year-old cycad.
☎ 625 90 21 🖥 www .dehortus.nl ✉ Plantage Middenlaan 2 € €6/3
🕐 9am-5pm Mon-Fri, 10am-5pm Sat & Sun (to 9pm Jul & Aug) ♿ good

Museumplein (4, B3)
This vast, open park behind the Rijksmuseum was cleverly redeveloped in 1999–2000 and today is one of Amsterdam's busiest open spaces. Beneath the park is a carpark and a supermarket, while back on the street level, there is a café, skate ramp, and in winter, an ice-skating rink.
✉ Paulus Potterstraat
🕐 24hr ♿ excellent

SKATING ON THIN ICE...
How much do the Dutch love ice skating? Well every year as winter arrives, brave, foolhardy or inebriated ice skaters hit the snap-frozen canals with predictable results. But as soon as winter really sets in there's no stopping the locals, who'd skate on a frozen bucket of water. To play it safe, head to the small skating rink at Museumplein (4, B3) where you won't get your feet wet.

A MAGICAL MOCHA MYSTERY TOUR

In 1690 the Dutch smuggled a coffee plant out of Yemen. Nurtured in the Hortus Botanicus (opposite) in 1714 a descendant was presented to Louis XIV. After successfully growing at the Jardin des Plantes in Paris, a plant was smuggled to Martinique. Brazil, which had no coffee plants, mediated in a 1727 coffee-growing border dispute between French and Dutch Guiana. A Brazilian officer, Colonel Francisco Melo de Palheta managed to both solve the conflict and seduce the French governor's wife who presented Palheta with flowers – and some secretly hidden coffee beans and seedlings. Today Brazil is the world's largest coffee producer.

Oosterpark (1, E4)

Oosterpark was laid out in the 1880s to accommodate the nouveaux riches of the city's diamond traders who had recently become wealthy from South African diamonds. The park makes a fine diversion if you're heading to the nearby Tropenmuseum (p16).
✉ 's-Gravesandestraat
☽ dawn-dusk ♿ excellent

Sarphatipark (3, E4)

This lovely little English country-style park was named after the tireless 19th-century philanthropist Samuel Sarphati (see p34) whose statue is front and centre in the park. It's a charming spot for a picnic lunch (or a sunbake in summer!) amid the many ponds, fountains and cute but voluble ducks.
✉ Ceintuurbaan ☽ dawn-dusk ♿ excellent

Wertheim Park (5, A5)

Opposite the Hortus Botanicus gardens is this intimate niche – often overlooked by tourists. Its most significant feature is its Auschwitz Monument designed by Dutch writer Jan Wolkers. This touching work featuring a split urn, embedded in the ground, containing ashes of Jews who died in Buchenwald concentration camp.
✉ Plantage Parklaan
☽ dawn-dusk ♿ excellent

Westerpark (1, C2)

Northwest of the Jordaan, the lovely Westerpark area, with its paths and shrubbery, connects to the Westergasfabriek Culture Park, with its excellent landscape architecture. Architecture buffs should combine this with a trip to Het Schip (p29).
✉ Haarlemmerweg
☽ 24hr ♿ excellent

QUIRKY AMSTERDAM

Hash Marihuana & Hemp Museum (2, D5)

While it makes sense that Amsterdam has a museum dedicated to *Cannabis sativa*, it's a ramshackle affair. Despite some interesting facts, such as the roots of marijuana use (first recorded in China in 3727 BC), the hodge-podge nature of the museum detracts from what's on offer.
☎ 623 59 61 ⌨ www.hashmuseum.com ✉ Oudezijds Achterburgwal 148 € €5.70 ☽ 11am-10pm ♿ good

Kattenkabinet (2, B8)

One strictly for cat lovers, this museum is devoted to the feline form in art. Founded in memory of the founder's cat (John Pierpont Morgan), the museum is as notable for the lovely building it's housed in as for the feline-focussed art.
☎ 626 53 78 ⌨ www.kattenkabinet.nl ✉ Herengracht 497 € €5/2.50

Make a feline for Kattenkabinet

THE GOOD DOCTOR

Amsterdam in the mid 19th century was a shadow of its former self; poor, debt-ridden and suffering from epidemics, in part due to the lack of sanitation. Enter one Dr Samuel Sarphati (1813–66), doctor, chemist and visionary. Sarphati set about tacking health concerns by initiating Amsterdam's first rubbish collections. Committed to health and education issues, he founded Holland's first bread factory as well as establishing trades and business schools. If that wasn't enough to fit into a short life, he built the prestigious Amstel InterContinental (p101) and the Palace of People's Industry (which burnt down in 1929 on the site of today's Nederlandse Bank).

🕑 10am-2pm Tue-Fri, 1-5pm Sat & Sun ♿ fair

Max Euwe Centrum
(4, B2)

This chess centre is dedicated to Max Euwe (1901–81), the Netherlands' only world chess champion (1935–7). Along with a permanent chess history exhibition, you can take a game with a computer or another player. Outside there is an oversized chess set where you can be publicly humiliated.
☎ 625 70 17 💻 www .maxeuwe.nl ✉ Max Euweplein 30a 🕑 10.30am-4pm Tue-Fri & first Sat each month ♿ poor

Poezenboot (2, C2)

On this houseboat on the Singel, cats actually appear to like water! The 'Catboat Foundation' looks after stray and unwanted cats, having them spayed, neutered and hopefully adopted out. The *Poezenboot* (cat boat) survives on donations and the love of the volunteers who work there.
☎ 625 87 94 💻 www .poezenboot.nl ✉ across from Singel 40 € donations encouraged 🕑 1-3pm ♿ fair

Sexmuseum Amsterdam
(2, D3)

Having reached the tender age of 21, what can the 'venustemple' provide that you can't see just walking Amsterdam's streets? While the sex shops offer you the latest, greatest ways to get off, the Sexmuseum is a temple to titillation through the ages that will provide more sniggers than serious contemplation. Visitors must be 16 years old or over.
☎ 622 83 76 💻 www .sexmuseumamsterdam .nl ✉ Damrak 18 € €3 🕑 10am-11.30pm ♿ fair

AMSTERDAM FOR CHILDREN

Children are most welcome in Amsterdam at tourist attractions and in pubs and restaurants. Many special events geared towards kids take place throughout the year. Check the monthly *Uitkrant* listings magazine under 'Agenda Jeugd'; otherwise contact the **Amsterdam Uit Buro** (4, B1; ☎ 0900-91 91 100, per min €0.40; Leidseplein 26) for special children's events.

Aviodrome Schiphol
(6, E3)

This national aviation museum provides an opportunity for children to learn how flight is achieved, use a flight simulator and sit at the controls of an Antonov AN-2 – which thankfully never leaves the ground. There's an impressive aircraft collection and you can book a short flight (phone ahead).

Chess can be a heavy game at Max Euweplein

☎ 406 80 00 🖳 www
.aviodrome.nl ✉ Schiphol
Centre, Westelijke Randweg
201 (Schiphol Airport)
€ €14.50/12.50 ⏰ 10am-
5pm Tue-Sun (until 6pm
Jul-Aug) ♿ excellent

Madame Tussaud's (2, C5)
After a €4 million 'facelift',
the weekend lines outside
Tussaud's attests to its
popularity. At least it's more
interactive these days, but
themes such as shopping
and dressing like J Lo and
being a model are pretty
lame. Still, don't miss your
only chance to see 'Bono' not
talking.
☎ 622 92 39 🖳 www
.madame-tussauds
.com ✉ Dam 20 (by Peek
& Cloppenburg) € adult/
under 5yr/5-15yr €17.75/
free/12.75 ⏰ 10am-5.30pm
♿ excellent (phone ahead)

Mirandabad (1, D5)
A wave machine, a beach,
elaborate slides and indoor
and outdoor pools *should*
be enough to keep toddlers
happy for a day at this
'aquatic centre'.
☎ 646 44 44 ✉ De Mi-
randalaan 9 € €3.40/2.60
⏰ phone ahead ♿ good

Tropenmuseum Junior
(1, E4)
The fascinating Tropen-
museum boasts a section

OTHER KIDDIE FAVOURITES
• Artis Zoo (p22)
• Canal cruises (p114)
• NEMO (p24)
• Vondelpark (p20)

for six- to 12-year-olds,
mostly in Dutch but offering
English-language programs
from June to September (call
ahead for times and prices).
Their aim is to promote
intercultural understand-
ing, with great hands-on
exhibits. (The admission
fee is in addition to the
Tropenmuseum admission;
see p16.)
☎ 568 82 33 🖳 www
.kindermuseum.nl
✉ Linnaeusstraat 2
⏰ 1-6pm Wed, 11am-6pm
Sat & Sun ♿ excellent

Tun Fun (2, F7)
In 2003 this former traffic
underpass was transformed
into a fun indoor play-
ground – perfect for rainy
Amsterdam days. Kids aged
one to 12 can build, climb,
roll, draw, play indoor
soccer and dance, while
parents can relax in the
café. Kids must be accom-
panied by an adult.
☎ 689 43 00 🖳 www
.tunfun.nl ✉ Mr Visserplein
7 € adult, child under
1yr/child1-12yr free/€7.50
⏰ 10am-6pm ♿ good

BABY-SITTING
Baby-sitters charge from €5 per hour, and there's often an additional €4 to €5 for
weekend nights. Agencies tend to use university students (female and male). Try **Op-
pascentrale Kriterion** (☎ 624 58 48; Roetersstraat 170; ⏰ 9-11am & 4.30-8pm),
the best known in town. Some upmarket hotels also offer baby-sitting (see listings in
the Sleeping chapter, p99).

Trips & Tours

WALKING TOURS
Historic Architectural Amble

At Dam Square admire the architecture of the **Koninklijk Paleis** (**1**; p30) before visiting **Nieuwe Kerk** (**2**; p26). Cross Nieuweziijds Voorburgwal to the Singel. Stroll by the old merchants' houses. Turn left into Korte Korsjespoortsteeg,

> **Distance** 2.5km **Duration** 2hr
> ▶ **Start** Koninklijk Paleis (p30)
> ● **End** Villa Zeezicht (p71)

crossing the bridge to Herengracht to the **Multatuli Museum** (**3**; p24). Head right into Roomolenstraat to the Singel to gape at the **grand 17th-century houses** (**4**). Turn left onto Brouwersgracht to the footbridge to view the elegant row of **16th-century houses** (**5**) in front of you. Continue along Brouwersgracht to **Het Papeneiland** (**6**; p83) for a break. Walking along Prinsengracht, turn right into Tuinstraat, and left into Eerste Egelantiersdwarsstraat where you can enter a covered passage to explore a **17th-century courtyard** (**7**). Continue down Egelantiersgracht passing **'t Smalle** (**8**; p83), then cross the Leliegracht bridge to Prinsengracht to visit **Westerkerk** (**9**; p31). Follow the waterfront, crossing Keizergracht to Leliegracht to admire the pretty **18th-century shopfronts** (**10**). Walking south on Herengracht you'll come to the **Golden Bend** (**11**), named after the wealthy merchants who lived in these grand 17th-century canal houses. Take Raadhuisstraat across to the Singel, turning left to finish at **Villa Zeezicht** (**12**; p71) for Amsterdam's finest apple pie.

Dress to match the Delft-blue tiles at Het Papeneiland (p83)

Sex, Drugs & Rock'n'Roll

Best undertaken at night, begin at the red-light district's gateway at **Oude Kerk** (**1**; p18), whose patron saint watches over prostitutes. Turn left onto Oudezijds Voorburgwal to the **Prostitution Information Centre** (**2**; De Wallenwinkel, Engestraat 3) to learn more about the world's oldest profession. Cross Korte Niezel, turning right onto Oudezijds Achter-

burgwal for the **Erotic Museum** (**3**; Oudezijds Achterburgwal 54). In the heart of the red-light district is the notorious erotic theatre **Casa Rosso** (**4**; Oudezijds Achterburgwal 106-108), famous for its live sex shows, and the **Hash Marihuana & Hemp Museum** (**5**; p33). Turn right into Oude Doelenstaat and check out **Greenhouse** (**6**; p94). Suitably more relaxed, head back across the bridge and left onto Oudezijds Achterburgwal where you'll see some **red lights** (**7**) and girls at work in their windows. Turn right into little Molenstraat, lined with more **red-light booths** (**8**). On Zeedijk, Amsterdam's Chinatown, stop in for tasty Chinese at **Nam Kee** (**9**; p64). Continue along Zeedijk to Warmoesstraat and for a beer at **In't Aepjen** (**10**; p82) before heading down wild **Warmoesstraat** (**11**), home to gay bars that hold sex parties and S&M nights. When you arrive at the **Winston International** (**12**; p89), you'll probably be in the mood for more beers and some loud rock'n'roll.

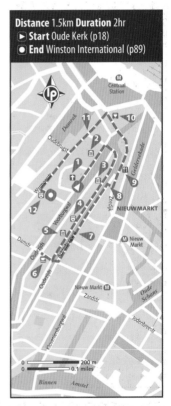

Distance 1.5km **Duration** 2hr
▶ **Start** Oude Kerk (p18)
● **End** Winston International (p89)

Under the red sky: a display at the Prostitution Information Centre

Nine Streets Shopping Saunter

If Amsterdam's ferocious mosquitoes are biting, start on Prinsengracht at specialised mosquito-net shop **Klamboe** (**1**; p60). If not, just admire the many shades and styles – same goes for the silk handbags next door at **Claire V** (**2**; p52). Cross to Reenstraat for culinary-focused gift shop

What's Cooking (**3**; p59). Across on Hartenstraat you'll find fascinating amusements at **The Gamekeeper** (**4**; p57) and on Gasthuisstraat is quirky **Brilmuseum** (**5**; p59). Take Singel to **Au Bout du Monde** (**6**; p54) for books on philosophy and spirituality, then to Oude Spiegelstraat. Call into **Urban Picnic** (**7**; p60) for specialised picnic gear or to order a picnic basket for your Vondelpark outing. On Wolvenstraat stock up on sensual specialities at **Zinne & Minne** (**8**; p61) and on Berenstraat browse handmade books by artists at **Boekie Woekie** (**9**; p55). Stroll across the bridge to **La Savonnerie** (**10**; p53) for organic soaps made on the premises, then back across to Prinsengracht and down to Runstraat to **Dutchies** (**11**; p52) for special edition leather handbags, and **Skins** (**12**; p54) for niche brand perfumes and cosmetics. Lastly, hit Huidenstraat to design your own funky jewellery at **Beadies** (**13**; p53), and while they're made to order eat a well-deserved lunch at **Lust** (**14**; p69).

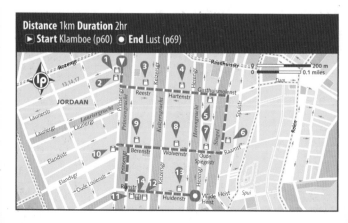

Distance 1km **Duration** 2hr
▶ **Start** Klamboe (p60) ● **End** Lust (p69)

Southern Canal Belt Stroll

If you want to get off the beaten track, wander down to the Southern Canal Belt early one evening – while it's short on sights, it's big on authentic atmosphere. Start on the **corner of Leidsestraat and Prinsengracht (1)** and stroll along Prinsengracht by the beautiful canal houses to **Niuewe Spiegelstraat (2)**. This charming street is crammed with wonderful antique shops and art galleries – head right to check out the fascinating shops on this block before returning to explore the area between Prinsengracht and Keizersgracht. Back on Prinsengracht, turn left and continue along the canal, admiring the gorgeous homes. **Le Zinc ... et Les Autres (3**; p75) is a special restaurant that you may want to book for another night. Continue ahead and stop on **Reguliersgracht bridge (4)** to savour the sublime views in all directions. Across the bridge, **Janvier (5**; p85) is a lovely place for a drink under the plane trees, where you can watch the local kids kick a football around on the Amstelveld. This is one of Amsterdam's most delightful spots. Head to **Utrechtsestraat (6)**, a low-key eat street, and try **Vooges (7**; p76), then have a beer with the locals at characterful pub **Oosterling (8**; p85).

Nothing but blue skies on Prinsengracht

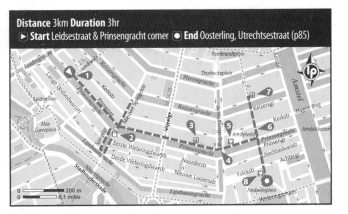

Distance 3km **Duration** 3hr
▶ **Start** Leidsestraat & Prinsengracht corner ● **End** Oosterling, Utrechtsestraat (p85)

DAY TRIPS
Haarlem (6, E2)

Some travellers actually prefer Haarlem to Amsterdam. Beautiful Haarlem has managed to do a better job at maintaining more of its 17th-century heritage and architecture than Amsterdam, and its historic edifices, leafy *hofjes* (courtyards) and old-world antique shops give the centre a real sense of history and grandeur. Its pretty bridges and winding alleys are just as charming as any in Amsterdam.

If you arrive by train your first sight will be Haarlem Centraal train station, an Art Deco masterpiece and the most beautiful in the country. As you walk to the centre along Kruisstraat, the wealth and elegance of the locals will become immediately apparent by the exclusive stores, art galleries and antique shops.

Lined with lovely cafés and restaurants, the Grote Markt is dominated by the magnificent late-Gothic Grote Kerk (aka Sint Bavokerk). Home to a wonderful Müller organ – once played by a 10-year-old Mozart – which is said to be the most splendid in the world.

Haarlem has two excellent museums that can be visited in a day. A short stroll south of Grote Markt, the Frans Hals Museum, in an almshouse where the painter spent some poverty-stricken years, is a must-see for fans of Dutch painting. It features many of the master's famous group portraits as well as works by other greats, including Jacob van Ruysdael and Pieter Brueghel the Younger. The Teylers Museum, the oldest museum in the country (1778), has an eclectic collection displaying everything from drawings by Michelangelo and Raphael to intriguing 18th-century inventions.

INFORMATION

10km west of Amsterdam

- 🚆 15min by train (every 15min) from Amsterdam Centraal
- 💻 www.haarlem.nl
- ℹ️ VVV (☎ 0900-61 61 600; Stationplein 1; per min €0.50); Frans Hals Museum (☎ 023-511 57 75; Groot Heiligland 62; €5; 🕐 11am-5pm Mon-Sat, 1-5pm Sun); Keukenhof (☎ 025-246 55 55; Stationsweg 166a, Lisse; €8/4.50; 🕐 8am-7.30pm late Mar-late May); Teylers Museum (☎ 023-531 90 10; Spaarne 16; €5.50/1.50; 🕐 10am-5pm Tue-Sat, noon-5pm Sun); Grote Kerk (Grote Markt; 🕐 10am-4pm Mon-Sat)
- ✕ De Haerlemsche Vlaamse (☎ 023-532 59 91; Spekstraat 3)

Leiden (6, E3)

Lively Leiden is a typical university town, home to the country's oldest university (founded in 1575), whose alumni include the great philosopher Descartes, and more than 20,000 students.

The university was a gift to the city from William the Silent (William of Orange) for withstanding a long Spanish siege in 1574. One-third of the residents starved before the Spaniards retreated on 3 October. The date is still celebrated as the annual town festival.

The great Dutch painters Rembrandt van Rijn, Jan Steen and Jan van Goyen were all from Leiden, yet the city has only one Rembrandt painting. Leiden boasts having more historic sights than any other city in the country, and most of these lie within a web of graceful canals, a 10-minute stroll southeast of the train station. The town has 11 first-class museums, including the Rijksmuseum van Oudheden (National Museum of Antiquities), which has a world-renowned collection of Greek, Roman and Egyptian artefacts, the pride of which is the extraordinary Temple of Taffeh, a gift from former Egyptian president Anwar Sadat to the Netherlands for helping to save ancient Egyptian monuments from flood.

> ## INFORMATION
> *40km southwest of Amsterdam*
> - 🚆 35min by train (every 15min) from Amsterdam Centraal
> - 💻 www.leiden.nl
> - ℹ️ VVV (☎ 0900-61 61 600; Stationsplein 210; per min €0.50); Hortus Botanicus (☎ 071-527 72 49; Rapenburg 73; €4/2; ⏱ 10am-5pm, closed Sat Oct-Feb); Rijksmuseum van Oudheden (☎ 071-516 31 63; Rapenburg 28; €4/2.50; ⏱ 10am-5pm Tue-Sat, noon-5pm Sun); Rijksmuseum voor Volkenkunde (☎ 071-516 88 00; Steenstraat 1; €4.50/3; ⏱ 10am-5pm Tue-Fri, noon-5pm Sat & Sun); De Valk (☎ 071-516 53 53; Tweede Binnenvestgracht 1; €4/3; ⏱ 10am-5pm Tue-Sat, 1-5pm Sun)
> - 🍴 De Hooykist (☎ 071-512 58 09; Hooigracht 49)

The Rijksmuseum voor Volkenkunde (National Ethnology Museum) focuses on the former Dutch colonies and the cultures of Asia, Africa, Latin America and the Middle East, much like Amsterdam's Tropenmuseum (p16), and has an exceptional Indonesian exhibition. The lush Hortus Botanicus, Europe's oldest botanical garden (1587), is home to the country's oldest descendants of the oldest Dutch tulips. It's a wonderful place to relax, with explosions of tropical colour and a fascinating steamy greenhouse.

INFORMATION
75km south of Amsterdam

- 🚆 1hr from Amsterdam Centraal
- 💻 www.rotterdam.nl
- € €12 return by train
- ℹ️ VVV (☎ 0900-403 40 65; Coolsingel 67; per min €0.50); Netherlands Architecture Institute (☎ 010-440 1200; Museumpark 25; €6.50; 🕐 10am-5pm Tue-Sat, 11am-5pm Sun); Museum Boijmans van Beuningen (☎ 010-441 94 00; Museumpark 18; €7; 🕐 10am-5pm Tue-Sat, 11am-5pm Sun); Kunsthal (☎ 010-440 03 01; Westzeedijk 341; €7.50; 🕐 10am-5pm Tue-Sat, 11am-5pm Sun)
- 🍴 De Engel (☎ 010-413 82 56; Eendrachtsweg 19)

Rotterdam (6, D3)

Rotterdam is the Netherlands' New York.

This vibrant city is home to some of the world's most adventurous, futuristic architecture. The Oude Haven (Old Harbour) is anything but old, with wonderfully imaginative structures, the most talked-about of which is the crazy Kijk-Kubu by Piet Blom. Rotterdam's Museum Park, designed by Rem Koolhaas, is home to five brilliant museums, and outdoor sculptures. The highly enjoyable Netherlands Architecture Institute is the most rewarding museum, the Kunsthal's modern collection of art, photography and design is the next, followed by the Museum Boijmans Van Beuningen.

Rotterdam has the Netherlands' most interesting and consistently good restaurants, along with hip bars and elegant grand cafés to rival Amsterdam's. Try the Oude Haven and Entrepot area.

The Hague (6, D3)

The Hague (Den Haag) may feel like a capital city – with its parliamentary buildings, grand boulevards and elegant embassies – but it's not. Amsterdam has been the capital since Napoleon took it away from The Hague in 1806.

INFORMATION
50km southwest of Amsterdam

- 🚆 50min from Amsterdam Centraal
- 💻 www.thehague.nl
- € €12 return by train
- ℹ️ VVV (☎ 0900-340 35 05; Koningin Julianaplein 30; per min €0.50); Binnenhof (☎ 070-364 6144; Binnenhof 8; €6; 🕐 10am-4pm Mon-Fri); Mauritshuis (☎ 070-302 34 56; Korte Vijverberg; €7; 🕐 10am-5pm Tue-Sat, 11am-5pm Sun); Gemeentemuseum (☎ 070-338 1111, Stadhouderslaan 41, €7.50; 🕐 10am-5pm Tue-Sat, 11am-5pm Sun)
- 🍴 WOX (☎ 070-365 37 54; Buitenhof 36)

Oddly, the administrative government is based in The Hague anyway. The UN's International Court of Justice is also there, along with other important international institutions, giving The Hague a big-city feel. Tours of the Binnenhof, the centre of Dutch politics, are available.

The world-class Mauritshuis museum has an impressive collection of the greatest Dutch and Flemish art, including renowned work by Rembrandt, Vermeer and Rubens, while the Gemeentemuseum is home to work by Piet Mondrian, MC Escher, Picasso and more. As you'd expect from such a city, there are some memorable restaurants and stylish bars.

Utrecht (6, F3)

Breathe in the history in the Netherlands's oldest city, picturesque Utrecht. A major political and religious centre during the Middle Ages, it had some 40 magnificent churches dotting the city. Today the French Gothic cathedral, the Domtoren, with 50 lovely bells, towers above the town. At 112m, it's the tallest in the Netherlands, and the views from the panoramic tower (stretching as far as Amsterdam) are spectacular.

The Centraal Museum has one of the Netherlands's most impressive collections of Golden Age art and is well worth a browse, while wandering along the city's tranquil 14th-century canals is also a must. Once chaotic working wharves, they're now home to elegant boutiques, interesting art galleries and stylish restaurants.

With one of the country's largest universities, and the student population to go with it, Utrecht's bars and cafés buzz till late most nights.

INFORMATION

40km southeast of Amsterdam

- 🚆 40min from Amsterdam Centraal
- 🖥 www.utrecht.nl
- € €7 by train
- ℹ VVV (☎ 0900-128 87 32; Vinkenburgstraat 19; per min €0.40); Centraal Museum (☎ 030-236 23 63; Nicolaaskerkhof 10; €8/4; ⏰ 11am-5pm Tue-Sun)
- ✖ De Winkel van Sinkel (☎ 030-251 06 93; Oudegracht 158)

Zaanse Schans (6, E2)

This kitsch open-air museum-village on the Zaan River is a bit of a guilty pleasure. It's undeniably touristy and tacky in parts, but it's picturesque because of its gardens and canal setting and can still be a lot of fun.

The six working windmills on the water are the highlight and apart from the villagers, who actually live and work here, are the most authentic things about the place. It was once the world's first light-industrial region, with more than 700 windmills powering flour and paint production.

INFORMATION

15km northwest of Amsterdam

- 🚆 20min from Amsterdam Centraal to Koog Zaandijk, then a 1km sign-posted walk
- 🖥 www.zaanseschans.nl
- € exhibits free
- ⏰ exhibits generally open 8.30am-5pm, but times vary so check the website; windmills open 8.30am-5.30pm Mar-Oct, weekends only Nov-Feb
- ℹ Information Centre (☎ 075-616 82 18; Zaanse Museum)
- ✖ De Kraai (no reservations)

The other buildings have been brought here from all over the country to re-create the 17th-century community and, understandably, some of them look out of place.

There are some fascinating exhibits on clog-making, cheese production, traditional handicrafts and pewter-work, and high-quality souvenirs are for sale.

ORGANISED TOURS

For those with limited time on their hands, a quick tour is not such a bad thing – it lets you see a whole lot of stuff in a short period so you can then decide where you'd like to return to spend more time. There's a tour to suit every taste in Amsterdam, ranging from bike rides to walking tours. Canal cruises are by far the most popular and are an absolute must. While some are themed (jazz, candlelight, pizza – you name it, they got it), some are simply practical, enabling you to get between many sights in a short time in the prettiest way possible.

City Tours

Keytours (2, D3)
Keytours is your one-stop-shop for city tours – on foot, bike, bus and boat – to all major sights. While its bus tours get you to sights you might not normally see (eg windmills), bus travel is the worst way to see the city. The tranquil two-hour candlelit cruise (€25) shows you the city at its loveliest.
☎ 623 50 51 ⌨ www.keytours.nl ✉ Damrak 19 € €8-55

Lindbergh Tours (2, D3)
While Lindbergh offers similar tours to Keytours, it also runs a city sightseeing bus tour with commentary, along with Rembrandt Tours, Red Light Tours and day trips out of Amsterdam, such as the Cheese Market and Windmill Tour (€27).

☎ 622 27 66 ⌨ www.lindbergh.nl ✉ Damrak 26 € €6.50-69

Red-Light District Tour (2, D3)
The Prostitutes Information Centre offers fascinating one-hour tours of the red-light district (11am on Tuesday, Wednesday and Friday), where it explains how the business works and you get to talk to a former prostitute about her work or the neighbourhood. Profits go back to the centre and reservations are necessary.
☎ 420 73 28 ⌨ www.pic-amsterdam.com ✉ Prostitutes Information Centre, De Wallenwinkel, Engestraat 3 € €15 🕒 6pm Fri & Sat

Urban Home & Garden Tours

From April to October these knowledgeable guides run popular excursions on Amsterdam architectural themes, taking you on tours of exteriors, homes and gardens, from monumental 17th-century churches to adventurous 21st-century museums.
☎ 688 12 43 ⌨ www.uhgt.nl ✉ Herengracht 605 € €23.50 incl drinks

Bicycle Tours

Cycletours Holland (2, A4)
If you'd like to combine an Amsterdam holiday with a cycling tour of the Netherlands, this company offers a number of tours by bicycle and barge boat (sleeping 15 to 30 people). The eight-day Top of Amsterdam tour leaves the city to cycle through the country's highlights.

☎ 521 84 90 ⌨ www.cycletours.com/tours ✉ Buiksloterweg 7 A € from €615 🕒 varies, check website

Let's Go (2, E2)
This excellent company gets rave reviews for their themed bike rides that include Tulip Bike Tours (€25, 4 ½ hours), self-guided Castle and Windmill Bike Rides, and an Amsterdam Mystery Tour that explores sites of secrets, legends, murders and public executions, hidden monasteries, lost public walls and more (€10, 90 minutes).
☎ 600 18 09 ⌨ www.letsgo-amsterdam.com ✉ VVV office, Centraal Station € €10-24.50 🕒 varies, check site

Mike's Bike Tours (3, C2)
Mike's four-hour standard tour scoots through the city highlights before heading out along the Amstel to visit a windmill, cheese farm, and clog factory, while the bike and boat tour gives more extensive coverage of the city with beer stops. You can also hire bikes for self-guide tours.
☎ 622 79 70 ⌨ www.mikesbikeamsterdam.com ✉ Kerkstraat 134; meet at entrance Rijksmuseum entrance, Museumplein, € €22 🕒 year round

Yellow Bike Guided Tours (2, C3)
Yellow Bike's city and countryside tours are fun, but their Segway tours are wild. The beauty of the Segway (as seen on the surreal comedy *Arrested Development*) is that

it can get to places bikes can't. After a 20-minute lesson, you glide through Amsterdam for two hours, giggling all the way.

☎ 620 69 40 🖥 www .yellowbike.nl ✉ Nieuwezijds Kolk 29 € €18-40 🕑 Apr-Nov

Boat Tours
Boom Chicago Showboat
(2, D2)

Boom Chicago, in conjunction with Lovers, offers an entertaining night, starting with a glam canal cruise on the luxe red-curtained Showboat to the Leidseplein dock. There you're met by Boom Chicago hosts and taken to the theatre for full VIP treatment, champagne, dinner, and the comedy show.

☎ 530 10 90 🖥 www .boomchicago.nl ✉ Central Station Prins Hendrikkade pier to Leidseplein 12 € €37.50 for 2 course meal & show/€58.50 VIP package, 🕑 5.30pm Wed Apr-Oct (depending on numbers)

Canal Bus & Bike

Amsterdam's most-used hop-on-hop-off canal service stops at 14 key tourist sights, including Central Station, Leidseplein, and all major museums, including

Anne Frank Huis and Rijksmuseum. A day pass is valid until noon the following day with unlimited use. It also rents the pedal-powered 'canal bikes'.

☎ 626 55 74 🖥 www .canal.nl ✉ offices at 14 stops € adult/child €17/11 🕑 May-Aug

Classic Boat Dinners
(3, B5)

Nothing gets more romantic than dining on this beautifully restored river launch, *Kleijn Amsterdam* (1905), as you cruise the quieter canals, personal waiter on hand, feasting on a gastronomic silver service six-course meal and marvellous wines. Propose during dessert and a yes is guaranteed.

☎ 330 19 10 🖥 www .classicboatdinners.nl ✉ Prinsengracht 391 € €80-190

GVB (2, E2)

GVB's ferry circuit takes in a number of Amsterdam sights, starting near Centraal Station and heading up the IJ River past the Eastern Islands. It also has hydrofoils and catamarans heading to other destinations. You can buy tickets from the GVB

office in front of Centraal Station.

☎ 460 53 53 🖥 www.gvb .nl ✉ Pier 8 De Ruijterkade € €7/5 🕑 varies

Lovers (2, D2)

While Lovers' hop-on-hop-off Museumboats (€15, including 50% off museum tickets) make life a whole lot easier, and its one-hour canal tour (€8.50) and candlelit cruises (€24) are exceedingly popular, its themed literary and architecture cruises are fascinating (€19.50).

☎ 530 10 90 🖥 www .lovers.nl in Dutch ✉ Central Station's Prins Hendrikkade pier € €8.50-75

Gay-Themed Tours
Historic & Hysteric Bicycle Tour (2, F2)

MacBike bicycle rental runs a self-guided gay and lesbian bicycle tour, providing you with a map and guide. The tour starts with a ride through the city's highlights (that's the historic bit) before heading through the gay entertainment streets of Warmoesstraat, Amstel and Reguliersdwarsstraat (the hysterical stuff).

☎ 620 09 85 🖥 www .macbike.nl ✉ Stationsplein 12 r € €1.50 🕑 any time

Shopping

Amsterdam's specialist stores are what make shopping the city so special.

Whether they specialise in cheese, olive oils, fine leather or natural soaps – or something quirkier, such as mosquito nets or juggling equipment – Dutch shopkeepers manage their businesses with pride. Their window displays are imaginative, their products beautifully presented, care and creativity are applied to gift-wrapping and service comes with a smile. Because many Dutch shop owners are managers and salespersons, their stores are like their homes. You're welcomed like a friend, often offered tea if you browse a while, and shopkeepers often share a bottle of wine out front at the end of the day. Their passion for their products is contagious: ask a question about a product and expect to spend time hearing about its history, where it was sourced and how long it took to make. You'll leave with three times as many as you'd intended to buy and return the next day!

None of this should be surprising – the Dutch have always been successful business people. During the 17th-century Golden Age, Amsterdam was the greatest trading city in the world. The Dutch East India Company was the world's first multinational and its ships brought back exotic goods from Asia, Africa and South America.

Amsterdam's best shops are in charming canal houses on cobblestone streets. This village-like atmosphere makes shopping a delight. The main shopping areas (see below) are manageable on foot. Major credit cards are accepted everywhere. Shopping hours vary, so are included in the listings below. Value-added tax (VAT) of 19% is included in prices. Non-EU visitors are entitled to a refund of VAT amounts over €150 (if purchased from a single shop on one day and exported within three months). Look for the Tax Free Global Refund signs, get a Global Refund Cheque from the shop, validate this at customs when you leave, and the supplier will refund your credit card or post you a cheque.

HOT SHOPPING AREAS

- Nine Streets, Jordaan (p38) – quirky specialised stores, funky boutiques, vintage clothes, homeware/design and music stores
- Haarlemmerstraat (2, B1) and Haarlemmerdijk (3, C1) – culinary street with quality sweets, pastries, cheeses, olive oils, Spanish delis, Asian supermarkets, book/record stores and offbeat boutiques
- Leidsestraat (2, A8) – upmarket fashion boutiques, designer shoes, perfume and cosmetics, souvenir stores and fast food
- Kalverstraat (2, B6) and Nieuwendijk (2, C4) – mainstream global brands, fashion franchises, department stores, music shops and endless mobile-phone stores
- Pieter Cornelisz Hooftstraat (4, B2) – luxury brands, exclusive fashion houses, designer shoes and jewellery stores, including Chanel, Gucci, Armani, Trussaardi, Cartier and Mont Blanc
- Nieuwe Spiegelstraat, Spiegelkwartier (4, D1) – antique stores, bric-a-brac, collectibles, tribal and oriental art, and commercial art galleries

DEPARTMENT STORES

Bijenkorf (2, C5)
Amsterdam's most popular department store is situated in a splendid building with stunning views from its café. It has lots of fabulous products on its five retail floors, from international designer brands such as DKNY to hip young Dutch labels such as G-Star.
☎ 621 80 80 ✉ Dam Square 1 🕑 11am-7pm Mon, 9.30am-7pm Tue & Wed, 9.30am-9pm Thu & Fri, 9.30am-6pm Sat, noon-6pm Sun

Hema (2, C4)
The Netherland's Hema is a cross between Kmart, IKEA, and a funky urban lifestyle store, with cheap, colourful, stylish stuff – everything from fashion basics and kid's clothes to cool homeware and Aussie wines.
☎ 623 41 76 ✉ Nieuwendijk 174 🕑 9.30am-6.30pm Mon-Wed, Fri & Sat, to 9pm Thu, noon-6pm Sun

Magna Plaza (2, B4)
This magnificent 19th-century building (p30), once

Magna Plaza: shopping on a grand scale

Smiles bloom at Bloemenmarkt

Amsterdam's main post office, is home to a marvellous upmarket shopping mall with over 40 stores – everything from Mango to Sissy Boy.
☎ 626 91 99 ✉ Nieuwezijds Voorburgwal 182 🕑 11am-7pm Tue-Sat, 10am-9pm Thu, noon-7pm Sun

Maison de Bonneterie (2, C7)
This grand, centuries-old, family-owned department store is where Amsterdam's establishment, including Queen Beatrix, likes to shop. Expect exclusive designer clothes and fine Italian shoes.
☎ 531 34 00 ✉ Rokin 140 🕑 noon-6pm Sun & Mon, 10am-6pm Tue-Sat, 10am-9pm Thu

Metz & Co (2, A8)
A very elegant department store, Metz is popular with well-heeled locals for its luxury goods, beautiful home décor and designer fashion.
☎ 520 70 36 ✉ Keizersgracht 455 🕑 11am-6pm Mon, 9.30am-6pm Tue-Sat, 9.30am-9pm Thu, noon-5pm Sun

MARKETS

Albert Cuypmarkt (4, D4)
Amsterdam's largest general market is home to some

wonderful, aromatic stalls selling Dutch cheese, olives, herbs and spices, and fresh fruit and vegetables. There are also stalls selling a lot of junk, fake leather, tacky souvenirs, and cheap luggage for those who've done too much shopping!
✉ Albert Cuypstraat 🕑 10am-5pm Mon-Sat

Bloemenmarkt (2, B8)
This colourful canalside flower market has been here since the 1860s, when gardeners used to sail up the Amstel and sell from their boats. This is the place to head to get your tulip bulbs and gardening accessories or to simply buy a bunch of flowers to brighten up your hotel room.
✉ Singel, btwn Koningsplein & Muntplein 🕑 10am-5pm Mon-Sat

De Looier (5, B5)
People either love or hate De Looier's hundreds of little stalls selling antiques, collectibles and bric-a-brac. You'll find everything from old furniture and Art Deco lamps to antique jewellery and delftware.
☎ 624 90 38 ✉ Elandsgracht 109 🕑 11am-5pm Mon-Thu, Sat & Sun

DUTCH TREATS

The best take-homes are uniquely Dutch products. Here's what to buy and where to get them:

- Tulip bulbs – nothing screams Netherlands more than tulips. At the Bloemenmarkt (p47) traders can give advice about restrictions on taking fresh bulbs home. Aussies and Kiwis (whose countries ban them altogether) should head to the Tulip Museum (p59) for gorgeous tulip-themed gifts.
- Diamonds – a diamond capital since Jewish diamond cutters arrived in 1585 fleeing persecution in Antwerp, Amsterdam is a great place to buy stones. Try the Amsterdam Diamond Center (p53) or Coster Diamonds (p53).
- Delftware – this blue-and-white pottery covered with a lustrous tin-oxide glaze was originally developed in the 1600s to imitate Ming dynasty porcelain. Buy your miniature windmills, clogs, and canal houses from Delft Shop (p59) or Galleria d'Arte Rinascimento (p59).
- Jenever – invented in the Netherlands by a Dutch alchemist in the 16th century, this strong gin-like spirit made with juniper berries was first used as a medicine! Le Cellier (p56) has a great range of smooth flavoured *jenevers*.
- Dutch Fashion – while not as famous in the fashion world as its Flemish sibling Antwerp, Amsterdam is starting to attract attention – discover up-and-coming talent at Young Designers United (opposite) or established eccentrics Viktor & Rolf at Van Ravenstein (opposite)

Oudemanhuis Book Market (2, D7)

A favourite with uni students and academics, this fascinating market, established in the 19th century, focuses on books, posters and postcards.
✉ Oudemanhuispoort
🕑 11am-4pm Mon-Fri

Waterlooplein (2, E7)

Amsterdam's most popular market is the place for second-hand clothes and vintage finds, Indian hippy gear, leather jackets, handicrafts and folk art from around the globe, gothic gear, bric-a-brac and drug paraphernalia.
✉ Waterlooplein 🕑 9am-5pm Mon-Sat

CLOTHING

Designer Gear

Cora Kemperman (4, C1)
No matter what the season, Amsterdam's Cora Kemperman's striking, whimsical, ethnic-inspired collections are defined by neutral colours and natural fabrics, crushed and crinkled looks, and lots of layers, volume and shape.
☎ 625 12 84
✉ Leidsestraat 72
🕑 noon-6pm Mon, 10am-6pm Tue-Sat, 10am-9pm Thu, noon-6pm Sun

Eva Damave (3, B5)

Eva Damave creates funky wool sweaters and zip jackets with her signature front patchwork panels made up of graphic cotton, silk and wool squares. She only produces one-offs or in small series, so you're unlikely to see anyone else wearing your woolie knit.
☎ 627 73 25 ✉ 2e Laurierdwarsstraat 51c
🕑 noon-6pm Wed-Sat

Laundry Industry (2, B7)

This cool Dutch label for men and women specialises in casual, functional fashion in neutral colours and natural fabrics. The name is a nod to the owners' earlier experience in wholesale clothing, where they spent much of their time laundering garments.
☎ 420 2554 ✉ Spuistraat 1, cnr Rokin 🕑 10am-6.30pm Mon-Sat, 10am-9pm Thu, noon-6pm Sun

Look Out (4, E2)

Looking through the racks at these wonderful neighbouring men's and women's stores is a real delight. Look out for super stylish labels such as Paul Smith, Philosophy, Etro, Kenzo, Bruuns Bazaar and Annemie Verbeke.
☎ 625 50 32 ✉ Utrechtsestraat 91 & 93 🕑 10am-6pm Tue-Sat, 10am-9pm Thu

Miaow (3, C5)

Analik is one of Amsterdam's edgiest young designers. Her latest enterprise, Miaow, is a showcase for her idiosyncratic collections, and like-minded labels such as Preen, Karen Walker, Kokon to Zai, and Henrick Vibskof. It also has changing exhibitions of graphic, media, graffiti and conceptual art.

☎ 422 05 61 ✉ Hartenstraat 36 ☪ 11am-6pm Mon-Sat

So Dutch Fashion (1, A4)

The Dutch Fashion Foundation promotes the best of Dutch fashion and helps designers develop their labels into commercial brands. Their showroom at the World Fashion Centre provides haute couture ateliers and carries collections by the hottest Dutch designers, such as Mada van Gaans, Jan Taminiau, Bas Kosters and Percy Irausquin.

☎ 617 09 57 ✉ World Fashion Centre, Wilhelminaplein 13, Tower 1, Floor 13 ☪ 10am-6pm Mon-Fri

Spoiled (4, C1)

At this one-stop-shop urban lifestyle store you'll find labels like Mads Norgaard, Rare, Junk De Luxe, Skunk Funk, True Religion, Stella Nova, My Ass, Fred Perry, Tommy Hilfiger and Tiger of Sweden, along with stylish shoes and accessories, cool magazines and art. You can also throw back an espresso and get your hair cut at H.I.P.

☎ 626 38 18
✉ Leidsestraat 27
☪ noon-6pm Sun & Mon, 10am-6pm Tue-Sat, 10am-9pm Thu

Van Ravenstein (3, C6)

At Gerda van Ravenstein's understated store, you'll find all the big names in Flemish design: Viktor & Rolf, Martin Margiela, Dirk Van Saene, Bernard Willhelm, AF Vandevorst, Walter Van Beirendonck, Veronique Branquinho, Ann Demeulemeester and Dries Van Noten.

☎ 639 00 67 ✉ Keizersgracht 359 ☪ 1-6pm Mon, 11am-6pm Tue-Sat

Young Designers United (4, C1)

Angelika Groenendijk-Wasylewski's boutique is a showcase for young Dutch designers. Check out Suzanne de Jager and Natasja Leenders' bold and playful Guten Appetit label, Heidi Long's striking collection, Marjoleine Innemee's Asian-inspired Minnemee, Ester Peters' fun Kinky Dream Wear, sexy Amber Rose, and Sarid Khomnoy's extravagant Amm Couture.

☎ 626 91 91 ✉ Keizersgracht 447 ☪ 1-6pm Mon, 10am-6pm Tue-Sat

Street Wear
Be Innocent (2, A6)

Style-savvy fashionistas will be familiar with these Victorian Gothic-inspired frilly baby doll dresses from the elegant Gothic Lolita look of the Japanese Harajuku sub-culture. Although it took off in Japan in the '90s, its recent appropriation by Gwen Stefani is now popularising it in the West.

☎ 320 59 87 ✉ Oude Spiegelstraat 9 ☪ noon-6pm Tue-Sat, noon-9pm Thu

City Slickers (2, A6)
This laid-back store with friendly staff is a great place to browse (to a grungy indie soundtrack) through racks of casual urban labels for men and women, such as Revolution, Red Rabbit, Itsus, Kuyichi, Emily the Strange and Lady Soul.
☎ 627 77 76 ✉ Wolvenstraat 8 🕑 11am-6pm Mon-Sat

Concrete (2, B6)
Part exhibition space showing rotating exhibitions of adventurous photography, graphics and illustration, and part cool clothes store. Features floating racks of zany Walter van Beirendonck t-shirts and jeans, Dutch labels Razk and D-Cent, along with interesting gear from Maharishi, Obey, Buddhist Punk, Michiko Koshino, Homecore and Minus Ung.
☎ 0900-262 73 83 ✉ Spuistraat 250 🕑 noon-7pm Mon-Sat, noon-5pm Sun

De Nieuwe Kleren van de Keizer (3, B6)
'The Emperor's New Clothes' has a funky range of club gear

and street wear from around the globe that guys won't find elsewhere in Amsterdam, including Pistol Pete (USA), Color Siete (Colombia), Tulio (Brazil), Ghanesh (Italy) and Priape (Canada). Other must-haves include Aerosol t-shirts, Unico underwear and Ulloa swimwear.
☎ 422 68 95 ✉ Runstraat 29 🕑 11am-6pm Tue-Sat

Exota (2, A5)
Head here for hip gear from indie labels such as King Louie and Aem Kei to global brands such as Kookai and French Connection. Also has kitsch accessories such as kooky dolly bags by local designer Olga Harbidge.
☎ 620 91 02 ✉ Hartenstraat 10 🕑 10am-6pm Tue-Sat, 10am-9pm Thu

TOP FIVE DUTCH DESIGNERS
Dutch fashion is strikingly idiosyncratic in its design. Here's our pick and where to find them.
• Analik – Miaow (p49)
• Viktor & Rolf – Van Ravenstein (p49)
• Cora Kemperman – Cora Kemperman (p48)
• Jan Taminiau – So Dutch Fashion (p49)
• Bas Kosters – So Dutch Fashion (p49)

Hana Zuki (4, D2)
Local designers started this funky boutique-come-studio as a showcase for their creations and those of their friends. Check out Hana Zuki's own graphic fashion, hip Aiko label, and edgy Phatoak by Dutch Natasja van den Elzen, along with illustrations, magazines, Lomos, and Maomaland's handmade toys.
☎ 422 95 63 ✉ Vijzelstraat 87 🕑 1-6pm Mon, 11.30am-6.30pm Tue-Sat

Henxs (2, E6)
The two tiny floors of this indie clothes store are crammed with fave labels of skaters and graffiti artists such as Hardcore, Bombers Best, Evisu and G-Star, along with graffiti supplies and edgy accessories.

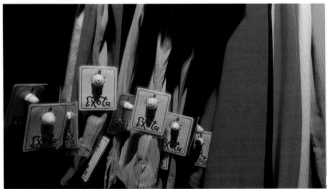
Exotic labels on blouses and shirts at Exota

Zip into Zipper for retro fashion

☎ 638 94 78 ✉ Sint Antoniesbreestraat 136 🕑 noon–6pm Sun & Mon, 11am–6pm Tue–Sat

Uri Duri (2, A7)
South Korean An-Su Kim's tiny boutique stocks funky little (little being the key word) dresses in retro fabrics that she designs and her mother and sister sew up in Seoul. These sassy numbers you won't find elsewhere are teensy – but they're worth dieting for!
☎ 422 94 57 ✉ Huidenstraat 30 🕑 noon–6pm

YOI (4, D3)
This 'hip honest guerrilla store' sells Dutch fashion produced with respect for humans, animals and the environment, made from organic cotton, hemp, secondhand clothes, recycled parachutes and prison blankets. Labels include fair trade threads by Fuck the Fashion, Lazy One, and This is a Story by Meike Beckers.
☎ 670 55 40 ✉ 1ste Jacob van Campenstraat 27 🕑 10am–6pm Tue–Sat

Second-Hand Gear
Episode (3, B5)
Visiting rock stars head to Episode to trawl through two floors of fabulous vintage and secondhand gear. Most impressive when we last dropped in were the seemingly endless racks of 1970s suede coats, folk peasant blouses, colourful ponchos and big, bright plastic sunshades.
☎ 626 46 79 ✉ Berenstraat 1 🕑 11am–6pm Mon–Sat

Lady Day (2, A5)
The vintage and second-hand clothes here are the kind you find in grandma's closet – lots of colourful cardigans and printed frocks. Beware, at first sight you think you've found the hottest thing yet and don't take it off for a season – next year it's hanging in the back of your closet.
☎ 623 58 20 ✉ Hartenstraat 9 🕑 11am–6pm Mon–Sat

Zipper (2,A7)
Amsterdam hipsters head here for seriously nostalgic, retro secondhand gear – wacky printed shirts, stove-pipe jeans, '40s zoot suits, porkpie hats and the like. There's also another store (2,A7; Huidenstraat 7).
☎ 627 03 53 ✉ Nieuwe Hoogstraat 8 🕑 11am–6pm Mon–Wed, Fri & Sat, to 9pm Thu, 1–5pm Sun

SHOES & HANDBAGS
Antonia By Yvette (2, A5)
These two canal houses are crammed to the rafters with fabulous shoes for men and women by Roberto Botticelli, Sonia Rykiel, Alberto Guardiani, Cavalli, Freelance and other international brands.
☎ 320 94 43 ✉ Gasthuismolensteeg 20 & Herengracht 243 🕑 10am–6pm Mon–Sat

Betsy Palmer (2, C5)
This funky orange-and-red-walled store is home to a

CLOTHING & SHOE SIZES

Women's Clothing

Aust/UK	8	10	12	14	16	18
Europe	36	38	40	42	44	46
Japan	5	7	9	11	13	15
USA	6	8	10	12	14	16

Women's Shoes

Aust/USA	5	6	7	8	9	10
Europe	35	36	37	38	39	40
France only	35	36	38	39	40	42
Japan	22	23	24	25	26	27
UK	3½	4½	5½	6½	7½	8½

Measurements approximate only; try before you buy.

Men's Clothing

Aust	92	96	100	104	108	112
Europe	46	48	50	52	54	56
Japan	S	M	M		L	
UK/USA	35	36	37	38	39	40

Men's Shirts (Collar Sizes)

Aust/Japan	38	39	40	41	42	43
Europe	38	39	40	41	42	43
UK/USA	15	15½	16	16½	17	17½

Men's Shoes

Aust/UK	7	8	9	10	11	12
Europe	41	42	43	44½	46	47
Japan	26	27	27.5	28	29	30
USA	7½	8½	9½	10½	11½	12½

mind-boggling range of cool yet very wearable women's shoes – from colourful beaded summery espadrilles to 1940s-style two-toned suede and leather court shoes. Their clogs are also very cool.
☎ 422 10 40 ⊠ Rokin 9 ⏲ 10.30am-6.30pm Mon-Sat, 1-6pm Sun

Claire V (3, B5)
The exquisite Claire V handbags are designed in Amsterdam but beautifully crafted by artisans in Vietnam and Cambodia using the finest hand-woven silks, beads and semiprecious stones. They also stock uber-fashionable Ipanima bags by Hong Kong–born Christina Yu, made famous by their *Sex and the City* appearances.
☎ 421 90 00 ⊠ Prinsengracht 234 ⏲ 11am-6pm Mon-Sat

Dutchies (3, B6)
Former lawyer Linda Creemers switched careers because she was frustrated that she couldn't find the kind of well-made leather handbags

that modern working women want – classic yet contemporary in design, in chic bright colours, roomy, durable and long lasting, and in limited editions so not every woman has one hanging on her arm.
☎ 626 30 01 ⊠ Runstraat 27 ⏲ 11am-6pm Tue-Sat

Hester van Eeghen (2, A5)
Designed in Amsterdam and handcrafted in Italy from fine leather, internationally renowned Hester van Eeghen's unique shoes are for those who dare to dress their feet dramatically in bright colour, fur, suede, and geometric patterns and prints. Her handbags are just as attention-grabbing.

☎ 626 92 11 ⊠ Hartenstraat 1 ⏲ 11am-6pm Tue-Sat

Seventyfive (2, E6)
One for true aficionados of sneakers, funky Seventyfive focuses on limited edition models, pilots, and rare trainers – and only stocks the very latest models of Nike, Puma, Adidas, ellesse, Cruyff, New Balance, Asics and Quick. Also at Van Woustraat 14 and Haarlemmerdijk 55.
☎ 626 46 11 ⊠ Nieuwe Hoogstraat 24 ⏲ 10am-6pm

Shoebaloo (4, B3)
The spaceship design of this futuristic store demands a

look – during the sales kick up your heels at discounts on shoes by Prada, Miu Miu, D&G, Gucci and Christian Dior. There are two other branches (2, A8; Leidsestraat).

☎ 671 22 10 ✉ Pieter Cornelisz Hoofstraat 80 ☷ 10am-6pm Tue-Sat, 10am-9pm Thu

JEWELLERY

Amsterdam Diamond Center (2, C5)
At Amsterdam's largest jewellery store you can buy loose diamonds as well as dazzling jewellery. Pieces include exquisite Bulgari diamond rings, Piaget diamond-encrusted watches, elaborate Chopard necklaces, elegant Mikimoto pearls and other wonderful extravagances.

☎ 624 57 87 ✉ Rokin 1-5 ☷ 10am-6pm Mon-Sat, 10am-8.30pm Thu

Beadies (2, A7)
Once the funky jewellery in the window draws you in, you'll find yourself here for hours selecting gorgeous beads, gems, charms and trinkets to design your own necklaces and bracelets. Our advice: don't start from scratch – opt for a variation on Beadies' fab designs, the staff take just an hour to create them!

☎ 428 51 61 ✉ Huidenstraat 6 ☷ 11am-6pm Mon-Sat

Biba (2, E6)
This girlie store stocks a range of glam but affordable contemporary jewellery – ethnic-inspired Satellite,

eclectic brand Reminiscence, chunky tribal Les Gens du Sud and old-fashioned Zazou.

☎ 625 54 23 ✉ Nieuwe Hoogstraat 12 ☷ 11am-6pm Mon-Sat, 1-6pm Sun

Coster Diamonds (4, B3)
Founded in 1840, Coster is famous for having cut the Persian Koh-I-Noor diamond for the British Crown Jewels in 1852 and the dazzling pink Star of the South diamond for the 1855 World Exhibition in Paris. One of Amsterdam's oldest diamond factories still in operation, it's one you can trust.

☎ 305 55 55 ✉ Paulus Potterstraat 2-6 ☷ 9am-5pm

PERFUMES & COSMETICS

La Savonnerie (3, B5)
Aromatic La Savonnerie makes more than 80 natural soaps on the premises, as well as stocking wonderful soaps from around the world – from rustic Aleppan olive oil soap to gentle Belgian donkey milk soap – and an enormous range of loofahs, sponges, back-scrubbers, soap dishes, and great gift packs.

☎ 428 11 39 ✉ Prinsengracht 294 ☷ noon-6pm Tue-Fri, noon-5pm Sat

Rituals (2, B6)
The flagship store of this heavenly brand (now a

Coster Diamonds: just rock up

ETHICAL BUYS

Many of the good altruistic folk of Amsterdam are giving something back to the communities where they commission or source their products from. You can encourage ethical trading by buying at the following:

- Bloom (p58) – this Dutch-Indian couple ensures child labour isn't used in the production of their beautiful products and donates some of their profits to their family foundation, Stitching Jaipur, to rescue street children in Jaipur, India.
- Claire V (p52) – this husband and wife team run a foundation that ensures 10% of their profits go towards micro-financing, business training and funding for the Cambodian landmine victims and Vietnamese artisans who hand-craft their splendid silk handbags.
- Cora Kemperman (p48) – a percentage of profits operate Cora Kempermen's foundation, Stitching Amma, which provides medical care, education, language lessons and micro-financing for their factory workers in India and Romania.

successful global franchise) which produces sublime products centred on enlivening everyday cleaning, refreshing, relaxing and energising rituals – from bathing to washing the dishes! We especially love their Rice Scrub, Hammam Body Mud, and Lotus Massage Oil.
☎ 344 92 22 ✉ Kalverstraat 73 ☽ 9am-6pm Sun-Sat, 9am-9pm Thu

Skins (3, B6)
This fabulous store is the exclusive Dutch dealer for most of the niche brands on their sleek shelves: Aveda, Aesop, Philosophy, NARS, Bloom, Annick Goutal, Frederic Malle, L´Artisan Parfumeur and Serge Lutens, along with Mason Pearson hairbrushes. Try Amsterdam's Ray Simons' Rose and Diamond Age Erasing Oil.
☎ 528 69 22 ✉ Runstraat 9 ☽ 1-7pm Mon, 11am-7pm Tue-Fri, 10am-6pm Sat

MUSIC & BOOKS

Athenaeum (2, B7)
Amsterdam's intellectual hub attracts academics, artists, media, design and fashion types to its bookshop's excellent and adventurous selection – and its adjoining newsagency's range of quality cutting-edge international magazines, newspapers and guidebooks.
☎ 622 62 48 ✉ Spui 14-16 ☽ noon-5.30pm Sun & Mon, 9.30am-6pm Tue-Sat, 9.30am-9pm Thu

Au Bout du Monde (2, A6)
Sit at the same table where Ringo Starr once philosophised, and join in on the engaging discussions encouraged by the warm staff at this welcoming shop specialising in books on every type of religion and philosophy, or, as they prefer, on the 'Old Age'.

☎ 625 13 97 ✉ Singel 313 ☽ 1-6pm Mon, 10am-6pm Tue-Sat

Au Pied de Terre (4, A2)
The city's best specialist travel and adventure bookshop is joining forces with its rival, Jacob Van Wijngaarden, to create the city's most comprehensive store with an enormous range of travel guides, literature, maps and globes.
☎ 627 44 55/612 19 01 ✉ 135-137 Overtoom ☽ 1-6pm Mon, 10am-6pm Tue-Sat

Blue Note (2, C4)
Blue Note is Amsterdam's specialist jazz store, with a wide range of international

jazz, blues and soul recordings, and a smaller section of acid jazz.
☎ 428 10 29 ✉ Gravenstraat 12 🕙 11am-7pm Mon-Sat, noon-5pm Sun

Boekie Woekie (3,B5)
This fascinating store focuses solely on books by artists, including self-published titles, handmade books, and monographs by local and international artists.
☎ 639 05 07 ✉ Berenstraat 16 🕙 noon-6pm Mon-Fri

Boudisque (2, D3)
Amsterdam's coolest independent music store has an great range of CDs and vinyl across all genres, with a generous selection of hip hop, reggae and world music and one of the finest art-house and animé DVD offerings anywhere.
☎ 623 26 03 ✉ Haringpakkerssteeg 10-18 🕙 noon-6pm Sun & Mon, 10am-6pm Tue-Sat, 10am-9pm Thu

Concerto (4, E2)
Spread over several buildings, this is the city's most engaging music store. It has an eclectic collection of new and second-hand records, CDs, DVDs and videos, with particularly good selections of opera and classical music.
☎ 623 52 28 ✉ Utrechtsestraat 52-60 🕙 10am-6pm Mon-Sat (to 9pm Thu), noon-6pm Sun

English Bookshop (3, B5)
This independently owned bookshop has the best range of Dutch literature and books on Amsterdam available in English. There's also a basement full of children's books and a terrific selection of quality fiction for when you run out of holiday reading.
☎ 626 42 30 ✉ Lauriergracht 71 🕙 10am-9pm Thu, 10am-6pm Fri-Sat, 11am-5pm Sun

Lambiek (2, A9)
Claiming to be the world's oldest comic store, Lambiek has been in operation since 1968 and stocks an impressive range of underground comics, newspaper strips, web comics and even erotic comics, along with classics such as Tintin, Asterix and Disney.
☎ 626 75 43 ✉ Kerkstraat 132 🕙 11am-6pm Mon-Sat, 1-5pm Sun

AMSTERDAM READS
- *Amsterdam: A Brief Life of the City (2001)* – Geert Mak
- *The Embarrassment of Riches (1987)* – Simon Schama
- *The Dutch Republic in the 17th Century (2005)* – Maarten Prak
- *Amsterdam: A Traveler's Literary Companion (2001)* – Manfred Wolf (ed)
- *Blue Mondays (2005)* – Arnon Grunberg
- *In Lucia's Eyes (2005)* – Arthur Japin

Whatever your poison, you'll find it at Le Cellier

FOOD & DRINK

De Bierkoning (2, B5)
Ignore the drunks who often down beers on the pavement out front (or join them!) – this is the city's best beer shop, with hundreds of beers from the Netherlands, Belgium, Germany and other big beer-making countries, along with branded beer mugs and glasses, and books about brewing.
☎ 625 23 36
✉ Paleisstraat 125
🕑 noon-6pm Mon, 9am-6pm Tue-Sat

De Kaaskamer (3, B6)
This wonderful cheese shop is the best in town and specialises in a wide variety of Dutch and other delicious cheeses, olives, tapenades, salads and other great picnic ingredients. You try before you buy and they're happy to make up cheese baskets to take home.
☎ 623 34 83 ✉ Runstraat 7 🕑 noon-6pm Mon, 9am-6pm Tue-Fri, to 5pm Sat, noon-5pm Sun

Geels & Co (2, D4)
The distinguished Geels & Co has been roasting wonderfully pungent coffees and selling aromatic loose-leaf tea for 140 years (since long before Warmoesstraat became the sleazy strip it is today). You'll also find charming teapots, coffee pots and brewing paraphernalia.
☎ 624 06 83 ✉ Warmoesstraat 67 🕑 9.30am-6pm Mon-Sat

JG Beune (3, C1)
This elegant sweet shop with original antique fittings has specialised in pastry and chocolate making since 1882. Buy a box of delicious rich milk chocolates in the shape of *Amsterdammertjes*, the cast iron spikes around the city that protect you from traffic (which was horse and wagon traffic back when these treats were first created!).
☎ 624 83 56 ✉ Haarlemmerdijk 156-58 🕑 10am-6pm Mon-Sat

Le Cellier (2, B4)
You'll find a splendid selection of Dutch *jenevers*, absinthe, spirits, liqueurs, a super range of Old and New World wines and around a hundred beers.
☎ 638 65 73 ✉ Spuistraat 116 🕑 11am-6pm Mon, 9.30am-6pm Tue-Sat

Meeuwig & Zn (2, B1)
Amsterdam's olive oil specialist supplies the city's best restaurants with delicious high-quality olive oils from Spain, Italy and Greece. They also sell mustards, mayonnaises, balsamic vinegars, tapenades, pestos, pâtés, harissa, fungi porcini and sea salt, so you're guaranteed to find something that fits in your carry-on.
☎ 626 52 86 ✉ Haarlemmerstraat 70 🕑 11am-6pm Tue-Sat, noon-5pm Sun

Papabubble (3, C1)
This funky sweet shop run by effervescent Mika and Dominik makes delicious sweets in-store. There's a

range of mouthwatering flavours, from kiwi to spicy cinnamon, but our favourite is lavender – you'll swear you can smell it when you taste it!

☎ 626 26 62 ✉ Haarlemmerdijk 70 🕙 noon-6pm Mon, 10am-6pm Tue-Sat

Puccini Bomboni (2, D7)
This wonderful chocolate-maker specialises in enormous truffles of the most unusual natural flavours, such as thyme, pepper, anise, cinnamon, apple and tamarind. Breathe in those aromas – yes, they're made on the premises!

☎ 626 54 74 ✉ Staalstraat 17 🕙 noon-6pm Mon, 9am-6pm Tue-Sat

FOR CHILDREN

De Beesten Winkel (2, D7)
This wonderful zoo of a store boasts the largest collection of cuddly exotic animals from around the globe. The owner makes it her mission to track them down, so to speak.

☎ 623 18 05 ✉ Staalstraat 11 🕙 1-6pm Mon, 10am-6pm Tue-Sat

Exota (3, B4)
Kids clothes don't get much cooler than this: funky little T-shirts, hippy-style print dresses, bohemian chic crocheted knits, and groovy lollypop-striped socks.

☎ 420 68 84 ✉ Nieuwe Leliestraat 32 🕙 1-6pm Mon, 10am-6pm Tue-Sat

The Gamekeeper (2, A5)
For older kids and adult kids at heart, this games shop is crammed with everything

from traditional games such as mah jong, chess and dominoes, to old family favourites such as Boggle and Dutch Monopoly, and nerdy brain teasers and card-based strategy games.

☎ 638 15 79 ✉ Hartenstraat 14 🕙 noon-6pm Sun & Mon, 10.30am-6pm Tue-Sat

Joe's Vliegerwinkel (2, E6)
Whether you're looking a kite for the kids that flies in nice patterns or you're after something more skilful and powerful, head to this specialised kite shop where you can also buy materials to build your own kites.

☎ 625 01 39 ✉ Nieuwe Hoogstraat 19 🕙 1-6pm Mon, 11am-6pm Tue-Sat

ARTS, ANTIQUES & COLLECTABLES

Decorativa (4, D1)
One of the city's most atmospheric antique stores, Decorativa is so cluttered with candelabra, costumes and crystal chandeliers that it's eccentric owner has put the paintings on the ceiling – look up!

☎ 320 10 93 ✉ Nieuwe Spiegelstraat 9A 🕙 noon-6pm Tue-Fri, 11am-5pm Sat

Eduard Kramer (4, C2)
Specialising in collectibles rather than antiques, this is another store that's crammed with lots of interesting stuff – if these objects could talk! Wonderful old wall and floor tiles, silver candlesticks, crystal decanters, antique jewellery and old-fashioned pocket watches.

☎ 623 08 32 ✉ Nieuwe Spiegelstraat 64 🕙 10am-6pm Mon-Sat, noon-6pm Sun

EH Ariëns Kappers (4, C2)
If you're looking for a special souvenir, then consider investing in one of the splendid Dutch etchings, prints, lithographs, or maps – from the 17th to the 20th centuries – from this elegant established store.

☎ 623 53 56 ✉ Nieuwe Spiegelstraat 32 🕙 11am-5pm Tue-Sun

DESIGN & HOMEWARE

Butler's (3, B6)
The luxury bathroom products in this plush store – velvety Missoni bathrobes and towels, Frette linen, Betula waterproof hamam thongs, DeLuxe spa products, candles and soaps – make you want to head back to the hotel and run a bath.

Fabricate your family tree with props from Decorativa

We love the Ex Voto Monsoon Tea Home Fragrance. ☎ 676 47 60 ✉ Runstraat 22 ✹ 11am-6pm Tue-Sat

BeBoB Design (4, D2)
Lovers of international 20th-century design classics – from Arne Jacobsen Swan chairs to Isamu Noguchi lampshades – should make this their first stop in Amsterdam. While they arrange shipping, a George Nelson ball clock should fit nicely in the carry-on. ☎ 624 57 63 ✉ Prinsengracht 764 ✹ noon-6pm Tue-Fri, 11am-5pm Sat

Droog@home (2, D7)
Droog means 'dry' in Dutch, as in 'dry wit', and Droog Design's products are strong on humour, concept and function. Martijn van der Pol's solid stainless steel sofa appears crumpled and Nina Farkache's 'Come a little bit closer' bench is topped with marbles that slide you up against your neighbour!

☎ 523 50 59 ✉ Staalstraat 7b ✹ noon-6pm Tue-Sun

Frozen Fountain (3, B6)
Head here for the best international product, furniture, lighting, textile and ceramic design brands, from Driade to Edra, plus great Dutch products. Owners Dick Dankers and Cok de Rooy contribute to the growth of local talent by showcasing designers and commissioning pieces. Look out for limited editions and serial products. ☎ 622 93 75 ✉ Prinsengracht 645 ✹ 1-6pm Mon, 10am-6pm Tue-Fri, 10am-5pm Sat

WonderWood (2, D6)
Specialising in classic and vintage plywood furniture from the '40s through to the '60s, along with limited Dutch editions, this is the place to head for funky chairs by Arne Jacobsen or Charles and Ray Eames, or Marchel Breuer Isokon nesting tables. ☎ 625 37 38 ✉ Rusland 3 ✹ noon-6pm Wed-Sat

GIFTS & SOUVENIRS

Bazar (2, C3)
If you collect kitsch souvenirs or want to buy the boys on the bucks night some gifts (so they don't go blabbing back home), then this is the place to head for the widest range of ridiculous tourist trinkets (see opposite) – everything from rude-shape egg fryers to fluffy clog slippers. ☎ 638 44 04 ✉ Nieuwendijk 128 ✹ 9.30am-10pm

Bloom (3, B4)
If hippy skirts and tie-die shirts come to mind when you think of Indian products, then you'll be wonderfully surprised when you see Bloom's exquisite shirts, jackets, bath robes, baby clothes and bed sets made out of the finest quality cottons, linens and silks. Also has high-quality handicrafts. ☎ 320 11 76 ✉ Prinsengracht 272 ✹ 1-6pm Mon, 11am-6pm Tue-Sat, noon-5pm Sun

IT'S GOT YOUR NAME ON IT
And if it hasn't, that won't take long to fix in Amsterdam!
- Pop into La Savonnerie (p53) in the morning to place your order and the next day you can pick up organic scented soaps with your name on them.
- Blond (opposite) can personalise their zany ceramics in a day, while orders made from scratch (ordered via their website www.blond-amsterdam.nl) take a month.
- Impress your friends with elegant embossed personal stationery, your own rubber stamp or a monogrammed seal from de Posthumuswinkel (opposite) – allow a week.
- Design your own fabulous beaded necklaces and gorgeous charm bracelets at Beadies (p53) and one hour later they'll be gracing your limbs for all of Amsterdam to covet. You can also order online at www.beadies.com.
- Local girl Linda Creemers at Dutchies (p52) does custom-made handbags in fine leathers and chic colours and can ship them home to you.
- Commission a Dutch-designed sculpture by Marc Ruygrok or furniture from Piet Hein Eek from Frozen Fountain (above) and have it shipped home.

TOP FIVE SOUVENIRS

If you're looking for a conversation starter (or stopper!), here are some ideas:
- A cannabis leaf grinder disguised as a miniature soccer ball (in Dutch colours).
- Fluffy clog-like slippers – get extra pairs for your guests to wear!
- A *flessenlikker* (bottle-licker) – a Dutch invention for getting that last bit of jam/honey/Vegemite from the bottom of the jar.
- Miniature glow-in-the-dark marijuana leaves for your bedroom ceiling.
- Any one of Amsterdam's array of silly phallic souvenirs (penis-shaped party whistles/wine bottle stoppers/novelty pens/Delft salt-and-pepper shakers/wind-up walking toy).

Blond (2, A7)

Blond is run by some cheerful blonde Dutch women who create colourful art, greeting cards and diaries, make fun fashion and accessories, and hand-paint cheery designs onto ceramics in-store.
☎ 428 49 29 ⌧ Singel 369 ◷ 11am-6pm Tue-Fri, 11am-5pm Sat

Delft Shop (4, C1)

This canal house store has a huge range of original blue-and-white delftware by Heinen Delftware (one of the last traditional centuries-old makers), Royal Porceleyne Fles and Royal Tichelaar Makkum, so you can sleep at night knowing your miniature clogs are the real deal.
☎ 627 82 99 ⌧ Prinsengracht 440 ◷ 9.30am-6pm Mon-Sat, 11am-5pm Sun

Miniature wooden clogs

Galleria d'Arte Rinascimento (3, B4)

Another charming canal house crammed with original delftware in every conceivable form: bowls, dishes, cheese plates, teapots, tiles, vases, egg cups, candlesticks, kissing cousins, clogs, chickens, horses and more.
☎ 622 75 09 ⌧ Prinsengracht 170 ◷ 9.30am-6pm Mon-Sat

Tulip Museum (3, B3)

There's a small but fascinating museum downstairs, and the ground-level shop has a wide range of tulip bulbs and tasteful tulip-themed souvenirs – from beautiful ceramics intricately decorated with tulips to elegant coasters, cards and cushion covers.
☎ 421 00 95 ⌧ Prinsengracht 112 ◷ 10am-6pm

What's Cooking? (3, B5)

The Dutch are imaginative dinner party guests. Instead of giving a bottle of wine or bunch of flowers to their hosts, they head here for more creative gifts, from colourful clip-on cooking timers to kooky-patterned oven mitts and polka-dotted flamenco-style kitchen aprons.
☎ 427 06 30 ⌧ Reestraat 16 ◷ 11am-6pm Tue-Sat

SPECIALIST & QUIRKY STORES

Brilmuseum (2, A5)

The 'Museum of Spectacles' displays 700 years' worth of frames in this charmingly cluttered store. It sells authentic unworn vintage frames – everything from Buddy Holly to Jackie O styles – for collectors and those who just like to stand out in a crowd.
☎ 421 24 14 ⌧ Gasthuismolensteeg 7 ◷ noon-5pm Wed-Sat

de Posthumuswinkel, Druwerken en Stempels (2, B6)

Looking for an original gift or souvenir? In the business of producing elegant personalised stationery, rubber stamps, and monogrammed seals since 1865, de Posthumuswinkel's range of *stempels* (stamps) is impressive. Orders take up to a week.
☎ 625 58 12 ⌧ Sint Luciënsteeg 23-25 ◷ noon-5pm Mon, 9am-5pm Tue-Fri, 11am-5pm Sat

Juggle Store (2, D7)

Don't even think of going anywhere else for your juggling needs. The Juggle Store has it all: glow-in-the-dark rings, colourful clubs,

DELFTWARE

While the Chinese get a lot of criticism for knock-off European designer gear, the blue-and-white Delft pottery, or delftware (see p48), was originally a Dutch imitation of fine Chinese porcelain. During the Golden Age of the 1600s, the Dutch East India Company, impressed with Chinese craftsmanship, imported the Chinese porcelain. Demand was so great that soon entrepreneurial Dutchmen from the town of Delft decided to start reproducing the Chinese products. While they initially copied the delicate Chinese styles featuring pretty landscapes, they soon developed their own patterns incorporating windmills and local scenery. These days, delftware comes in a mind-boggling array of forms, from splendid vases to miniature clog trinkets. In Amsterdam the kissing gay cousins are a big seller.

bean-filled balls, fire torches, diabolos, yo-yos, unicycles, Chinese spinning plates, top hats and scores of books and videos for learners.
☎ 420 1980 ✉ Staalstraat 3 ⏱ noon-5pm Tue-Sat

Klamboe (3, B4)
Mosquitoes are ferocious in Amsterdam, with victims (these writers included) testifying to their deadly bites and lasting scars. Locals are smart – they shop at Klamboe and cover their beds with beautiful mosquito nets in a range of bright colours and styles, from casual chic to easy elegance.
☎ 622 94 92 ✉ Prinsengracht 232 ⏱ 11am-5pm Tue-Sat

Nieuws (3, B4)
A mind-boggling array of kooky trinkets cram this entertaining store – from quirky action figures (we love the Crazy Cat Lady, the Obsessive Compulsive, Rosie the Riveter and Albino Bowler!) to mini-patron saints, foreplay dice and voodoo dolls. Travellers love the Wash Away Your Sins Soap.
☎ 627 95 40 ✉ Prinsengracht 297 ⏱ 1-6.30pm Mon, 11am-6.30pm Tue-Sun

Santa Jet (2, A2)
Forgot to pack your love potion? Lost your good luck charm? Or just plain out of prayer candles? This delightful store is stuffed with endless spiritual kitsch and Latin American folk art to decorate a Day of the Dead department store window in Mexico City.
☎ 427 20 70 ✉ Prinsenstraat 7 ⏱ 11am-6pm Mon-Fri, 10am-5pm Sat

Urban Picnic (2, A6)
Amsterdam's canalside seats and parks are wonderful for picnics – this is the place to come for colourful plastic picnic sets and baskets, tiny foldable tables, mats to sprawl out on, teensy tin barbecues and delicious 'picnics to go' with sandwiches, salads, quiches, cake and wine!
☎ 320 88 66 ✉ Oude Spiegelstraat 4 ⏱ 9am-6pm Mon-Sat

RECREATIONAL DRUGS

'Smart drug shops' sell legal organic hallucinogens such as magic mushrooms, herbal ecstasy, marijuana seeds, mood enhancers and aphro-disiacs – those trying them for the first time should follow the dosage advice.

Elements of Nature (2, D3)
Amsterdam's slickest smart shop stocks psychedelic herbs, pills, seeds, energy boosters, stimulants and hemp products. Khat (smoked in Yemen) and Cloud Herb (claiming to invoke Aztec visions) come recommended, as do multi-drug urine testing kits (to see if you have anything to be nervous about at work on Monday!).
☎ 421 58 85 ✉ Haringpakkerssteeg 11-13 ⏱ 11am-10pm

Kokopelli, Conscious Dreams (2, D3)
Mexican shaman accessories, hallucinogens such as San Pedro cactus, a greenhouse where you can learn to grow your own, a cloud lounge with water views, and a DJ on weekends are what sets this smart drug shop in the Red Light District apart from the rest.
☎ 421 70 00 ✉ Warmoesstraat 12 ⏱ 11am-10pm

Magic Mushroom Gallery (2, B6)
The array of fresh magic mushrooms is mindboggling

USE IT OR LOSE IT!

There's more to ganja than just smoking it – you can eat it too! These fun foodstuffs are available all over Amsterdam – just don't try to take them home, they *do* contain marijuana.

- hemp lollypops
- ganja leaf rock candy
- cannabis instant coffee
- hemp chocolate
- canna biscuits

but staff are on hand to give advice. You'll find Flower Power herbal ecstasy, the euphoric sassafras root and Shamandance (a hypnotic combination of damiana, wormwood and passionflower that 'opens new roads to dreams and imagination') among other herbal blends.

☎ 427 57 65 ⊠ Spuistraat 249 🕑 11am-10pm Sun-Thu

SEX SHOPS

You might never have been to a sex shop before, and probably won't visit one again, but it's an absolute must in Amsterdam, where the stores are often clean and sleek and the titillating products are stylishly displayed. Go for a giggle or an original gift.

Absolute Danny (2, D5)
This is considered to be Amsterdam's finest erotic and

fetish clothing store, with rubber and PVC dominatrix gear their specialty. They also sell hard-core videos and magazines, and tickets to fetish events.

☎ 421 09 15 ⊠ Oudezijds Achterburgwal 78 🕑 11am-9pm Mon-Sat, noon-9pm Sun

Female & Partners (2, B4)
Run by two women, this elegant erotic store was Amsterdam's first aimed at women and their partners. There's a wide selection

of sexy lingerie and body jewellery designed by the pair, along with the usual leather, rubber, PVC, vibrators, kinky toys, books and DVDs.

☎ 620 91 52 ⊠ Spuistraat 100 🕑 1-6pm Mon, 11am-6pm Tue-Sat, 11am-9pm Thu

Mr B (2, D4)
Gay guys around the globe swear by Mr B's leather emporium for the best S&M range, rubber gear and bondage accessories. They also sell DVDs, magazines, and Pride paraphernalia, from flags to stickers, and have an online store.

☎ 422 00 03 ⊠ Warmoesstraat 89 🕑 10am-6pm Mon-Sat, 10am-9pm Thu

Zinne & Minne (2, A6)
Women won't find this sensual store the least bit intimidating and its lovely owner Inez Reijbroek is happy to help or leave you to browse. Try Geisha's Secrets with essential love oils and tickle feathers, or the Kama Sutra Bedside Box with honey dust and massage oil.

☎ 330 34 82 ⊠ Wolvenstraat 14 🕑 11am-6pm Tue-Sat

Window-undressing at Female & Partners

Eating

Because Amsterdammers appreciate plain talk, we'll take this opportunity to state that Amsterdam is not one of the culinary capitals of the world. While the cuisine of the world's great cities – and Amsterdam *is* one – has either found new life with old recipes (Paris), found a way to attract fantastic chefs (New York), taken fresh produce and regional influences and made something special (Sydney) or just saw an opportunity to make pub food interesting again (London), Amsterdam still wonders why anyone would want something more sophisticated than a sandwich for lunch.

Having said that, Amsterdam's food scene *is* improving. While the Dutch have a national cuisine based on rudimentary meat, potatoes and vegetables (in that order), contemporary chefs are doing tasty variations on sober old Dutch dishes. Sophisticated French and Mediterranean restaurants are turning out great plates around the city. And when it comes to decent midrange meals, we salute the Thai, Indonesian and Chinese restaurants of Amsterdam.

This isn't to say you can't eat well in the city's cafés and bars. In winter, *stamppot* (hotchpotch) – mashed potatoes with raw or cooked vegetables nestled next to smoked sausage – is enviable comfort food. Sitting in the sun on a canal with a decent beer and some *kroketten* (croquettes) or anything eaten with a toothpick can be sublime. If herrings are in season, don't hesitate to try some. And you can't leave Amsterdam until you've tried the apple pie.

To avoid disappointment, just remember lunch is a 'bread and butter' meal and dinner is eaten early – most restaurant kitchens open from 5.30pm to 10pm, though diners tend to linger over drinks long after food service is finished. Opening hours, rather than food service times, are listed in this guide.

You don't get more Dutch than herring with onion and gherkin

Tongues wag outside De Waag, Nieuwmarkt

CENTRUM

Brasserie Harkema (2, C6)
International €€
This cavernous ex-tobacco factory started its career as a restaurant in fine fashion a couple of years ago. Now the hype has subsided, it's just a very good, stylish brasserie, with a simple lunch menu and uncomplicated brasserie staples such as Caesar salad and entrecôte for dinner.
☎ 428 22 22 ✉ Nes 67 ☽ 11am-1am (to 3am Fri & Sat) ♿ good

Café de Jaren (2, C7)
International €€
This big, buzzy and bright bar-café-restaurant is one of the city's best. It's the kind of place where you head for a good coffee and end up leaving hours later having consumed an entire magazine, a decent meal, a few glasses of wine and watched the boats and

beautiful people pass by on the terrace.
☎ 625 57 71 ✉ Nieuwe Doelenstraat 20 ☽ 10am-1am ♿ excellent ♿ V

Cafe in de Waag (2, E5)
International €€€
While good weather will see you seated outside to gawk at the market crowds, the interior of this historic building (p29) is a delight. The extensive lunch menu goes beyond the usual selection of sandwiches, while the dinner menu holds no surprises.
☎ 422 77 72 ✉ Nieuwmarkt 4 ☽ 10am-midnight ♿ fair ♿ V

d'Vijff Vlieghen Restaurant (2, A7)
Dutch €€€
Sure it's the place where tourists come when they want a 'quality' local meal. And of course, if you sit in the Rembrandt Room, camera-wielding visitors will lean over you to get a snap. Still, no-one in town treats Dutch

cuisine quite so well. Book ahead.
☎ 530 40 60 ✉ Spuistraat 294-302 ☽ 5.30-10.30pm ♿ good ♿ V

Frenzi (2, D7)
Mediterranean €€
After a Waterlooplein market (p48) shopping expedition, refuel at this nearby café-restaurant, which serves up excellent sandwiches, soups (an excellent fish soup) and pasta. At night, the menu is more sophisticated with a great tapas plate, satisfying mains and a good, short wine list.
☎ 620 84 58 ✉ Staalstraat 21 ☽ 8.30am-11pm Mon-Fri, 10am-11pm Sat & Sun ♿ good ♿ V

Green Planet (2, B4)
Vegetarian €€
While it looks like your average veggie restaurant (and that's no compliment), the food here is more hip than hippy. It's a globetrotting menu — expect anything from spinach and

PAYING THE BILL

Meal prices are average by European standards and servings are hearty – the Dutch love a filling meal. A service charge of 15% is usually included in the bill, and locals round off to the nearest euro or give a 5% to 10% tip, depending on the service. Reservations are often wise for anything grander than a café, and many smaller restaurants don't accept (or grudgingly accept) credit cards.

goat-cheese quiche to Indian curry – and of course it's all eco-friendly and organic.
☎ 625 82 80 ✉ Spuistraat 122 ☾ 5.30pm-midnight Tue-Sun ♿ excellent ♨ Ⓥ

Joselito (2, C2)
Spanish Tapas €€
While tapas is growing in popularity in Amsterdam, you'd swear most of the chefs cooking these tempting tasters had never set foot in España. Humble little Joselito, however, serves up some of the most authentic tapas around, with decent portions and an excellent outdoor terrace to take in *el sol*.
☎ 622 76 78 ✉ Nieuwendijk 2 ☾ 11am-11pm ♿ good Ⓥ

Kung Fu (2, B6)
Asian €€
Just the kind of funky and kitsch Asian place we like to drop in on. Killer cocktails (try their Hong Kong Sling with lychees) followed by great nibbles (dim sum) to line your stomach and, if you really settle in for the night, filling mains.
☎ 528 95 91 ✉ Rokin 84 ☾ 5pm-late Tue-Sun

Latei (2, E5)
International €
If at first sight you thought Latei was a secondhand shop selling '50s and '60s lamps

and trinkets, you would be correct. But what Latei also does is make some of the best coffee and snacks in Amsterdam. And, oddly enough, has very popular and fun couscous nights.
☎ 625 74 85 ✉ Zeedijk 143 ☾ 8am-6pm Mon-Wed, to 10pm Thu & Fri, 9am-10pm Sat, 11am-6pm Sun ♿ fair ♨ Ⓥ

Le Marche (2, C8)
Delicatessen €
Le Marche is popular with travellers heading off for a picnic and for its wonderful freshly squeezed juices and shakes. Choose from fantastic *panini* (sandwiches), quiches and freshly baked cakes, along with pastas, stir-fries and noodles. On the first floor, there's a light and airy sit-down cafe with wi-fi.
☎ 235 83 63 ✉ Vroom & Dreesmann Department Store, Kalverstraat 201 ☾ 10am-7pm Mon-Fri, 10am-9pm Sat, noon-6pm Sun ♿ fair Ⓥ

Luden (2, A7)
Brasserie €€
If you are tiring of eetcafé sandwiches, Luden serves up good value 'real' lunches from Monday to Friday. It's pretty standard brasserie fare, but the smoked duck breast with fruit sorbet and rocket is a standout, and

the cheese plate is a winner. Good wines and great Singel views.
☎ 330 56 70 ✉ Spuistraat 304-306 ☾ noon-midnight ♿ excellent ♨ Ⓥ

Nam Kee (2, E4)
Chinese €-€€
Closely followed by New King (opposite), this is our favourite Chinese restaurant in Amsterdam. It's certainly not for the décor, but for the brilliantly tasty roast duck and pork, and the fantastic soup they plonk them in. The oysters (steamed) are so famous here there's a book and movie named after them.
☎ 624 34 70 ✉ Zeedijk 111-113 ☾ noon-11pm ♿ excellent Ⓥ

Duck in for barbecued delights at Nam Kee

New King (2, E4)
Chinese €€
Like an upmarket version of its near neighbour Nam Kee (opposite), New King does some pretty fine Chinese food with added piped music and 'better' décor. Try the mixed dim sum, pork and duck dishes.
☎ 625 21 80 ✉ Zeedijk 115-117 ⏰ 11.30am-midnight ♿ excellent Ⓥ

Supperclub (2, B5)
International €€€€
Supperclub is a unique Amsterdam institution. Eating a set menu while propped up in a bed in an all-white room, while any manner of performances go on around you, may be your idea of a dream or a nightmare. Go anyway and be sure to wear nice socks.
☎ 638 05 13 ✉ Jonge Roelensteeg 21 ⏰ 8pm-1am Wed-Sat Ⓥ

Vasso (2, B7)
Italian €€€
Elegant, rustic and very chic, Vasso is a great Italian eatery just off hectic Spui. Delicious antipasti and filling pastas are the order of the day, and if you get to mains or dessert, we salute you.
☎ 626 01 58 ✉ Rozenboomsteeg 10-14 ⏰ 5-10pm

Supperclub: all brass

Vermeer (2, E3)
French €€€€
Vermeer has all the trappings of a Michelin-starred establishment: the booze cart, fussy flower arrangements and an air of reverence. After it lost a star (now down to one), this is the best time to visit as the kitchen is out to impress. Lobster, duck and sweetbreads regularly make appearances on the menu.
☎ 556 48 85 ✉ NH Barbizon Palace Hotel, Prins Hendrikkade 59 ⏰ noon-3pm Mon-Fri, 6-11pm Mon-Sat ♿ Excellent

JORDAAN

Balthazar's Keuken (3, B6)
French/Mediterranean €€
This refreshing little restaurant offers a fixed-price, three-course menu that often changes week by week, depending on what's best at the markets. As they're only open three days a week (make sure you book ahead), they appear to be more focussed on the food than most.
☎ 420 21 14 ✉ Elandsgracht 108 ⏰ 6-11pm Wed-Fri ♿ fair

FEBO
If you see FEBO (pronounced fay-bo) through your beer goggles or through a haze of spliff smoke, it starts to make sense. Why wouldn't you want hot croquettes or a hamburger that's been sitting forlornly in a little coin-operated glass shoe box? This Amsterdam fast food chain (branches everywhere – and we mean everywhere) also does fried chicken and fries and is enormously popular. And we don't have a problem with that. It's just that it's equally popular during the *day*. People, it's hot food from a coin-operated machine!

Blue Pepper (4, B1)
Contemporary Indonesian €€
Chef Sonja Pereira does contemporary Indonesian with Pacific Rim references like no-one else in Amsterdam. The stylish room is a delight, so sit back, order one of the well-chosen wines and one of the delicious set menus – which arrive well-paced, well-sized and packed with flavour.
☎ 489 70 39 ✉ Nassaukade 366 🕒 6-10pm 👤 good V

Bordewijk (2, A1)
French €€€€
Almost certainly your best bet for hearty French fare, Bordewijk's understated décor (book a table on the canalside terrace in summer) lets the food do the talking. Expect dishes such as *côte de bœuf* (beef steak) alongside truffles, oysters and duck.
☎ 624 38 99 ✉ Noordermarkt 7 🕒 6.30-10.30pm Tue-Sun 👤 excellent V

De Bolhoed (2, A2)
Vegetarian €€
An unrepentantly old-school, open-sandaled type of vegan eatery, De Bolhoed is the most popular vegetarian restaurant in town. Italian, Mexican and Middle Eastern dishes all make appearances, and yes, there's plenty of tofu. Service is friendly and the helpings generous.
☎ 626 18 03 ✉ Prinsengracht 60-62 🕒 noon-10pm (from 11am Sat) 👤 excellent ♿ V

Divan (3, B5)
Turkish €€
Hidden behind a brown-café façade, this great little restaurant serves up some of Amsterdam's best Turkish cuisine. Order some *meze* (mixed starters) and don't miss out on the lamb as a main course.
☎ 626 82 39
✉ Elandsgracht 14
🕒 5-11pm 👤 fair

Envy (3, B5)
International €€
Created by the Supperclub crew (p65) Envy is a hip, sleek, minimalist restaurant that encourages diners to take a five-course menu of seemingly endless, excellent tasters. While the concept works, Envy could do with more pride and less sloth, some of our 'warm' dishes arrived cold and no-one remotely cared. Now that's not hip.
☎ 344 64 07
✉ Prinsengracht 381

RESTAURANTS THAT MEAN BUSINESS
If you're in Amsterdam on business, impress your guests by suggesting the best restaurant for sealing a deal. The following restaurants are sure-fire signature-signers:
- Christophe (p68)
- Yamazato (p77)
- La Rive (p74)
- d'Vijff Vlieghen Restaurant (p63)
- Zuid Zeeland (p71)

🕒 5-11pm
👤 good V

Jean Jean (3, B3)
French €€-€€€
While it no longer attracts the hipsters, Jean Jean is a warm, stylish local restaurant serving up refined French comfort food such as *escargot* (snails) and rack of suckling pig.
☎ 627 71 53 ✉ Eerste Anjeliersdwarsstraat 14
🕒 6-10pm Tue-Sun

Moeder's Pot Eethuisje (3, C1)
Dutch €
If there is a more cluttered restaurant interior in Amsterdam, we haven't seen it. Endearing 'Mother's Pot' is best visited outside the summer months when the old-school favourites such as liver with onions and bacon,

and the classic *stamppot* make complete sense.

☎ 623 76 43 ✉ Vinkenstraat 119 ⏱ 5.30-9.30pm Mon-Sat ♿ excellent ♿

NOA (4, B1)
Asian €€€

'Noodles of Amsterdam' is certainly the hippest place in the city to enjoy some noodles. With its lounge feel and great cocktails, you might even forget to order some of the pan-Asian food coming out of the open kitchen. No great loss – the food is the least of the attractions here.

☎ 626 08 02 ✉ Leidsegracht 84 ⏱ 6pm-midnight Mon-Sat, from 1pm Sun ♿ excellent V

Proeverij 274 (3, B5) ✳
French/International €€

Beef carpaccio with bananas? Crème brûlée with foie gras? With a menu that reads like someone's been spending far too much time at an Amsterdam coffeeshop, Proeverij shouldn't work. But culinary adventurers will be rewarded here with some amazingly unexpected combinations served up in a casually romantic atmosphere.

☎ 421 18 48 ✉ Prinsengracht 274 ⏱ 6-10pm ♿ good

Raïna Raï (3, B5)
Algerian €

This little local delicatessen and café does everything from great dips to couscous with *merguez* (spicy sausages). You can eat in or take away.

☎ 624 97 91 ✉ Prinsengracht 252 ⏱ noon-midnight ♿ fair V

Rakang Thai (3, B6)
Thai €€-€€€

While the décor is a little odd at this venerable Thai eatery, it's so busy here that you won't mind grabbing the straightjacket-decorated chairs (no, really) when they become available. The relaxed service and wonderful authentic Thai food will keep you riveted to your seat.

☎ 627 50 12 ✉ Elandsgracht 29 ⏱ 6-10.30pm ♿ excellent V

Small World Catering (3, C1)
Snacks €

Just off the Haarlemmer shopping strip, this tiny café (part of a catering business) is the perfect place to stop and refuel. More takeaway than eat in, the food couldn't be fresher nor the coffee better. Try whichever quiche is on offer.

☎ 420 27 74 ✉ Binnen Oranjestraat 14 ⏱ 10.30am-8pm Tue-Sat, noon-8pm Sun ♿ excellent

Toscanini (3, C2)
Italian €€€

This Italian eatery has been seducing diners for years with its authentic Italian fare. What keeps them coming back is the fresh pastas, risotto cooked to order, organic and free-range meats, along with an admirably long Italian wine list (ask the sommelier for advice). Reservations essential.

☎ 623 28 13 ✉ Lindengracht 75 ⏱ 6-10.30pm ♿ fair V

You do make friends with salad at De Bolhoed

WESTERN CANAL BELT

Café Het Paleis (2, B5)
Café €€

This friendly little local attracts a 20–30-something crowd who covet the outdoor tables in good weather or crowd the communal table inside. The menu of sandwiches, bagels and ciabattas, along with a couple of pastas is fine, if not fascinating, and there are decent wines by the glass.
☎ 626 06 00
✉ Paleisstraat 16
🕒 10am-11pm 🚻 fair Ⓥ

Café Van Zuylen (2, B4)
Café €€

While we have developed an aversion to BLT sandwiches in Amsterdam, we'll forgive this café because sitting on the canalside terrace here, with its undergraduate vibe and *gezellig* atmosphere, is as good as it gets. So if it's a pleasant day, pull up a table

UNIQUE EATS
• Supperclub (p65) – have a good lie down
• Café-Restaurant Amsterdam (p76) – postindustrial imbibing
• Blue Pepper (p66) – Indonesian fine dining? Oh yes!
• De Kas (p77) – life is good in the greenhouse
• Bazar (p72) – Middle Eastern meze in a church

and soak it up. Maybe even order a sandwich.
☎ 639 10 55 ✉ Torensteeg 8 🕒 10am-10pm 🚻 fair

Café Walem (2, A8)
International €€

While not as fashionable as it once was, Walem has reached classic status for serving up decent light meals and great coffee for over 20 years. The service is notable as well, and if you're lucky enough to score good weather and a seat outside, you won't mind the occasionally inconsistent food.
☎ 625 35 44 ✉ Keizersgracht 449 🕒 10am-1am

Chez Georges (2, B3)
French €€€

It's best to set aside at least a couple of hours to dine at this intimate restaurant. Order the chef's menu and prepare to be blown away by a chef who really knows and loves his Burgundian cuisine. You'll probably have to book well ahead (there's only a few tables).
☎ 626 33 32 ✉ Herenstraat 3 🕒 6-10.30pm Mon-Tue, Thu-Sat

Christophe (3, C4)
French €€€€

This long-standing Michelin-starred restaurant is a firm favourite on every foodie's Amsterdam 'to do' list. Mixing the south of France with the Mediterranean, chef Jean-Christophe Royer's seasonal menu always demonstrates his deft touch with spices and seasonings, and the wine list has some great finds.
☎ 625 08 07 ✉ Leliegracht 46 🕒 6.30-10.30pm Tue-Sat 🚻 fair

Damsteeg (3, B5)
French/International €€€

A popular dinner choice in the Nine Streets area, Damsteeg is located in an attractive classic Amsterdam building with an elegant interior. While they specialise in fish dishes (they do a great

Crystalware at Christophe

Subdued lighting and glorious seafood at De Belhamel

bouillabaisse), the meat and vegetarian dishes are fine as well. They have a little tapas menu next door.

☎ 627 87 94 ✉ Reestraat 28-32 🕑 6-10.30pm 🚹 fair 🅅

De Belhamel (2, B1)
French/Mediterranean €€€
This pretty restaurant, located on one of the most scenic canal junctions in Amsterdam, has an Art Nouveau interior that is just as breathtaking as the view. The food does some neat hopping between French, Italian and Dutch, with seafood the hit of the main courses. Book an outside table in summer.

☎ 622 10 95 ✉ Brouwersgracht 60 🕑 6-10pm Sun-Thu, 6-10.30pm Fri & Sat 🚹 fair 🅅

De Struisvogel (3, B5)
French €€
An endearing little basement restaurant on Keizersgracht, De Struisvogel (The Ostrich) serves up honest fare – yes,

including ostrich dishes. The three-course blackboard menu changes regularly and is amazing value (€19).

☎ 423 38 17 ✉ Keizersgracht 312 🕑 6-11pm

Foodism (2, A4)
International €€
A good all-day café with friendly staff, Foodism serves up excellent breakfasts, filling sandwiches (try the goat cheese and chorizo) and hearty pastas. A good selection of vegetarian dishes too.

☎ 427 51 03 ✉ Oude Leliestraat 8 🕑 11.30am-10pm Mon-Sat, 12.30-10pm Sun 🚹 fair 🅅

Goodies (2, A7)
Café €€
A favourite stop on the Nine Streets, rustic Goodies is far more popular than you'd expect from the jumble sale of a day menu. At night, the pasta dishes keep it popular with locals.

☎ 625 61 22 ✉ Huidenstraat 9

🕑 9.30am-10.30pm Mon-Sat, 11am-4.30pm Sun 🚹 good 🅅

Letting (2, A2)
Café €€
A great all-day café, Letting attracts a steady procession of locals who ritualistically visit for a quick snack and a coffee. Alongside the ubiquitous *broodjes* (bread rolls) there are usually a couple of pastas on the menu. Check the daily specials too.

☎ 627 93 93 ✉ Prinsenstraat 3 🕑 8am-9pm 🚹 🅅

Lust (3, B6)
International €
Nothing to do with the ubiquitous sex shops of Amsterdam (*lust* is Dutch for appetite), simple salads and pasta dishes make this place a great refuelling stop on a shopping expedition. Busy for dinner as well as lunch.

☎ 626 57 91
✉ Runstraat 13
🕑 9.30am-11pm
🚹 excellent 🅅

Morlang (2, A8)
International €€
Along with Café Walem (p68) minimalist Morlang is a great spot for a casual snack during the day or more hearty fare at night. The overly eclectic menu features everything from wonton soup to Moroccan lamb, and the hipsters are happy with it – grab a canalside table and enjoy.
☎ 625 26 81 ✉ Keizersgracht 451 🕒 11am-1am

Pastini (4, C1)
Italian €€
This lovely canalside restaurant doesn't just rely on its picturesque location to draw in diners. From the mercifully uncomplicated menu, start with the antipasto and follow with whichever delicious fresh pasta takes your fancy. Desserts are divine and the wine list is a short trip through Italy. Book ahead.
☎ 622 17 01 ✉ Leidsegracht 29 🕒 6-10pm
♿ fair 🚻

Prego (2, A3)
French €€€
A pretty, simple, split-level restaurant, the chef here does some interesting and well-prepared takes on French cuisine. The menu is seasonal and the wine list short but intriguing. But be prepared for a long night – these are the most relaxed chefs we've ever witnessed in a restaurant kitchen.
☎ 638 01 48 ✉ Herenstraat 25 🕒 6-10pm ♿ fair

Pur Sang (2, B1)
International €€
A fine lunch stop during weekend shopping or for

BEST TERRACES IN TOWN
When the sun decides to visit, make a beeline for the following places:
• Café de Jaren (p63)
• Morlang (left)
• Café Van Zuylen (p68)

dinner, Pur Sang has a comfortable bar and an interesting menu to peruse while you wait. For dinner expect plenty of Mediterranean-style seafood – such as grilled sardines with salsa – risotto, and some decent vegetarian options.
☎ 330 26 28 ✉ Haarlemmerstraat 105 🕒 4pm-1am Mon-Thu, 11am-10.30pm Fri, 11am-2am Sat, noon-1am Sun ♿ good Ⓥ

Restaurant Vijf (2, A2)
French/Mediterranean €€€
This elegant restaurant has a simple formula of five starters, main courses and desserts, or a five-course tasting menu. The regularly changing menu is often filled with French classics, however more inventive dishes such as scallops with cucumber sorbet keep it interesting.
☎ 428 24 55 ✉ Prinsenstraat 10 🕒 6-10pm Tue-Sat

Singel 404 (2, A7)
Café €
In a super spot by a bridge, an appearance by the sun here is quickly followed by the appearance of every local in the know who wants to grab a bite and some rays at everyone's favourite lunch café. They do a huge range of sandwiches and great desserts.
☎ 428 01 54 ✉ Singel 404 🕒 noon-6pm ♿ excellent 🚻 Ⓥ

Spanjer en van Twist (3, C3)
International €€
Spanjer en van Twist's wonderful canalside tables overlooking the Leliegracht make it one of the best spots for watching the boats battle it out for canal space. Given this, you don't mind the occasionally slow service and sometimes overstretched, but tasty eclectic menu.
☎ 639 01 09 ✉ Leliegracht 60 🕒 10am-10pm

(to 11pm Fri & Sat)
☻ good ☻ V

Stout (2, C1)
Café €€-€€€
Funky and casual, Stout is your best bet for a stop along the Haarlemmerstraat shopping strip (p46). The lunch menu is interesting, but it's later when the locals drop in for tasting plates (the 'Stout Platter') that the place hots up.
☎ 616 36 64 ✉ Haarlemmerstraat 73 ☻ 10am-11pm Mon-Sat, noon-11pm Sun ☻ excellent V

't Buffet van Yvette & Odette (2, A6)
Café €
Sure there are BLTs on the menu at this wonderful light-filled café, but we'll forgive this because the 'breakfast complete' (with coffee, juice, croissant and

eggs) and the sticky toffee cake are so delicious.
☎ 423 60 34 ✉ Herengracht 309 ☻ 8.30am-5.30pm Mon-Fri, 10am-5.30pm Sat, noon-5.30pm Sun ☻ V

Top Thai (2, B3)
Thai €€
After a move to brighter but less enigmatic surrounds, thankfully the no-nonsense Thai menu and cooking remain intact. Go for the selection of starters, one of their spicy beef salads (very hot!) and the Pad Thai Gai (stir-fry noodles with chicken).
☎ 623 46 33 ✉ Herenstraat 28 ☻ 4-10.30pm ☻ fair V

Uyt (3, B6)
International €€
This smart little local spot in the Nine Streets district

(p46) is popular due to the kitchen's competent cooking and good value, three-course fixed price menu (€25.50). It's an eclectic one too – everything from Thai beef salad to lamb couscous – with an equally globe-spanning wine list.
☎ 627 06 18 ✉ Runstraat 17d ☻ 6-11pm ☻ fair

Villa Zeezicht (2, B4)
Café €
While Villa Zeezicht does some decent lunch items, it's all really clumsy foreplay for the homemade apple tart with cream that is a justifiable Amsterdam legend.
☎ 626 74 33 ✉ Torensteeg 7 ☻ 7.30am-9pm ☻ excellent ☻ V

Werck (3, B4)
International €€
This light, airy eatery just across from Anne Frank Huis (p10) attracts a fairly hip crowd who linger over brasserie staples such as salmon, duck breast and steaks. There is a lovely outdoor terrace and it gets very busy late when the DJ (Thursday to Saturday) starts spinning. Book ahead for dinner.
☎ 627 40 79 ✉ Prinsengracht 277 ☻ 10am-1am Mon-Thu, 10am-3am Fri & Sat ☻ V

Zuid Zeeland (2, A8)
French €€€
This refined, friendly restaurant is one of Amsterdam's most consistently good restaurants. In a city where many eateries appear to be suffering from bipolar disorder, Zuid Zeeland delivers the gourmet goods,

Spanjer en van Twist: a name and menu with a twist

with terrific terrines, soups and meat dishes. And any restaurant serving a 'real' lunch is fine by us.
☎ 624 31 54 ✉ Herengracht 413 ⏰ noon-3pm Mon-Fri, 6-11pm Ⓥ

DE PIJP & OUD ZUID

18 Twintig (4, D3)
International €€
This handsome eatery and bar on popular Ferdinand Bolstraat has a fascinating menu that often translates into some great eating. The food is very fresh, there are good wines by the glass and the DJ on Friday and Saturday nights adds to the hip atmosphere.
☎ 470 06 51 ✉ Ferdinand Bolstraat 18-20 ⏰ 5pm-1am Mon-Thu, 5pm-2am Sat & Sun ♿ good Ⓥ

Balti House (4, C4)
Indian €€
Locating decent Indian food in Amsterdam can be a trial, however this mid-sized eatery does a good job of sating cravings for an Indian feast. Head straight for the hotter end of the menu, where the kitchen excels, and grab a Kingfisher beer and an outside table if the weather is agreeable.
☎ 470 89 17 ✉ Albert Cuypstraat 41 ⏰ 4-11pm ♿ good Ⓥ

Bazar (4, E4)
Middle Eastern €
Our favourite break from the hectic Albert Cuypstraat markets, this authentic slice of the Middle East is amusingly set in a cavernous former church. The kitschy décor brings a smile to your face, the Arab pop soundtrack sets

GOOD TO GO
Places to go if you want something on the run:
- Khorat Top Thai (below)
- Raïna Raïl (p67)
- Singel 404 (p70)
- Small World Catering (p67)
- Wok to Walk (p76)

your fingers drumming and the food is well matched.
☎ 675 05 44 ✉ Albert Cuypstraat 182 ⏰ 8am-1am Mon-Thu, 8am-2am Fri, 9am-2am Sat, 9am-midnight Sun ♿ excellent 🚹 Ⓥ

Café Loetje (4, C4)
Café €€
Steak. And snarky service. If you don't like it, don't bother coming to this Amsterdammers' old favourite, because it's hard to escape either! Just order up a steak (it comes medium rare), salad and fries and you'll be eating like a local.
☎ 662 81 73 ✉ Johannes Vermeerstraat 52 ⏰ 11am-10pm Mon-Sat (no lunch Sat) ♿ fair Ⓥ

De Waaghals (4, C3)
Vegetarian €€
The 'Dare-Devil' will please vegetarians who want to be treated better than dining lepers in Amsterdam. A stylish but informal eatery, the menu changes regularly and uses plenty of organic ingredients (fantastic mushrooms), including wine.
☎ 679 96 09 ✉ Frans Halsstraat 29 ⏰ 5-9.30pm Tue-Sun ♿ excellent Ⓥ

De Witte Uyl (4, C3)
International €€€
A local favourite, Amsterdammers fill the tables spill-

ing along the footpath during summer. The eclectic menu sees diners choosing two dishes from around the dozen listed, plus a dessert, for a fixed price. The restaurant uses organic and free-range meat, vegetarians aren't forgotten, and there is a good by-the-glass wine selection.
☎ 670 04 58 ✉ Frans Halsstraat 26 ⏰ 6pm-1am Tue-Sat ♿ excellent Ⓥ

Khorat Top Thai (4, A2)
Thai €€
This casual little Thai place keeps very busy serving up decent helpings of Thai curries. Classics such as *tom kha gai* (chicken soup with coconut milk) are also pretty good. Take away is available.
☎ 683 12 97 ✉ 2e C Huygenstraat 64 ⏰ 4-10pm ♿ fair Ⓥ

Le Garage (4, B4)
French €€€
Once you appreciate that this red velvet and mirrors restaurant will be full of frozen-featured 'ladies who lunch' and local celebrities you won't recognise, you can concentrate on the imaginative *haute cuisine* coming out of the capable kitchen. If you can't be bothered dressing up, head next door to their more casual eatery.
☎ 679 71 76 ✉ Ruysdaelstraat 54 ⏰ noon-2pm Mon-Fri, 6-11pm ♿ fair

Le Hollandais (4, F4)

French €€€

This split-level restaurant is perfect for those who love good French regional cooking. There are plenty of (free-range) meat dishes on offer as well as game and shellfish (in season). Informed staff can help you select a great wine from the short but impressive wine list.

☎ 679 12 48 ✉ Amsteldijk 41 🕒 6.30-10.30pm Mon-Sat ♿ fair

Mamouche (4, D4)

Moroccan €€€

Stylish and minimalist, Mamouche brings Marrakesh cool, and countless hipsters, to de Pijp. The menu strays from classic Moroccan on occasion but is authentic where it counts, such as the lamb tagine and vegetable couscous.

☎ 673 63 61 ✉ Quelli-jnstraat 104 🕒 6-11pm ♿ fair Ⓥ

Patou (4, B3)

International €€

Patou is the perfect fit on PC Hooftstraat, where well-heeled shoppers burn up their credit cards. While the sandwich menu is the usual affair, mains such as the Wagyu beef burger are very popular.

☎ 676 02 32 ✉ PC Hooftstraat 63 🕒 8.30am-

9pm Mon-Sat, 10am-9pm Sun (kitchen closes 7pm) ♿ fair Ⓥ

Puyck (4, D4)

French/International €€

Nestled in among Amsterdam's computer shops, Puyck is an attractive restaurant serving up some interesting dishes that foodies will love. Expect seafood cooked with Asian and French influences and some fascinating desserts.

☎ 676 76 77 ✉ Ceintuur-baan 147 🕒 5.30-10.30pm Mon-Sat ♿ good Ⓥ

Restaurant Altmann (4, F4)

International €€€

An elegant restaurant, the valet parking gives a hint of what kind of clients unfurl their napkins here. The seasonal menu includes delectable dishes with a few Middle Eastern favourites (such as lamb with couscous) handled with a deft touch.

☎ 662 77 77 ✉ Amsteldijk 25 🕒 noon-2pm Tue-Fri, 6pm-midnight ♿ good Ⓥ

Spring (1, C4)

International €€€

This modish restaurant is unassuming from the outside, but inside it's stylish with an amiable atmosphere and good service. The menu, a mix of international and Mediterranean dishes (including a daily risotto), offers plenty of seafood and shellfish (in season). The cooking and presentation are refined, and the wine list substantial.

☎ 675 44 21 ✉ Willem-sparkweg 177 🕒 noon-2pm Mon-Fri, 6-10pm Mon-Sat ♿ good

Trèz (4, C4)
Mediterranean €€€
There's never a free table at this friendly restaurant. Stylish inside and packed outside during summer, try what everyone else has – the Trèz tapas platter – before tackling a meaty main course.
☎ 676 24 95 ✉ Saenredamstraat 39-41 🕑 6-10pm Tue-Thu & Sun, 6-11pm Fri & Sat ♿ excellent V

Zaza's (4, D4)
French/Mediterranean €€
This attractive little restaurant cites a connection with feeling 'Ab Fab', a reference to the TV series *Absolutely Fabulous* that is clearly lost in translation. Not lost in translation is the pretty fab food that materialises out of the tiny kitchen. Try the goat cheese entree and follow it with the lamb or duck.
☎ 673 6333 ✉ Daniël Stalpertstraat 103 🕑 6-10.30pm Mon-Wed, 6-11pm Thu-Sat ♿ fair V

SOUTHERN CANAL BELT

Coffee & Jazz (4, E2)
Indonesian €€
Along this busy eat street, this funky little joint excels in serving up simple Indo fare along with great jazz and smooth coffee. Simple, really.
☎ 624 58 51 ✉ Utrechtsestraat 113 🕑 9.30am-8pm Tue-Fri, 10am-4pm Sat ♿ fair V

La Storia Della Vita (4, D3)
Italian €€
If you're craving hearty Italian, this old-school restaurant is so authentic you half expect a mob hit while sipping your post-meal grappa. The brilliant *bresaola* (cured beef) and filling gnocchi almost take your mind off the piano music. On weekends, the set menus are worth booking for.
☎ 623 42 51 ✉ Weteringschans 171 🕑 6-11pm Mon-Sat ♿ good V

La Rive (4, F3)
French €€€€
Even after having a Michelin star burn out (it's down to one), La Rive is still one of Amsterdam's favourite 'special occasion' restaurants. With lovely views over the Amstel, refined French classics coming out of the kitchen and an eye-popping

COMFORT CUISINE
Some traditional Dutch dishes:
Appelgebak Warm apple pie with whipped cream.
Erwtensoep Thick pea soup with smoked sausage and bacon.
Kroketten Crumbed, deep-fried meat or shrimp-filled croquettes, served with mustard.
Pannenkoeken Large pancakes with ingredients such as bacon and cheese or apples and cherries.
Uitsmijter Fried eggs, ham and cheese on toast.

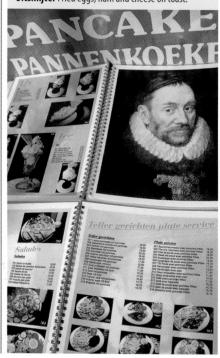

wine list, it's a memorable restaurant.

☎ 622 60 60 ✉ Professor Tulpplein 1 🕑 noon-2pm Mon-Fri, 6.30-10.30pm Mon-Sat ♿ excellent

Le Pêcheur (4, D1)
Seafood €€€
Why there aren't more great seafood restaurants in Amsterdam is a mystery, however, long-standing Le Pêcheur with its delectable seafood and lovely terrace certainly goes a long way to make up for this shortfall. Fantastic soups, shellfish and white wine list.

☎ 624 31 21 ✉ Reguliersdwarsstraat 32 🕑 noon-3pm Mon-Fri, 5.30-11pm Mon-Sat ♿ fair

Le Zinc...et Les Autres (4, D2)
French €€
This quaint and cosy old canal-house restaurant is a delightfully and unapologetically old-fashioned affair, as well as being quite a romantic address. The menu matches the vibe well – quality ingredients are cooked with care and there are some interesting wines to match.

☎ 622 90 44 ✉ Prinsengracht 999 🕑 5.30-11pm Tue-Sat ♿ fair Ⓥ

Piet de Leeuw (4, D2)
Dutch €€
A local favourite, this authentic eatery has been around forever serving up slices of cow to a return audience of meat-loving Amsterdammers. Besides the tender steaks, there is liver with bacon and onions as well as herring on toast. Comfort food never tasted so good!

☎ 623 71 81 ✉ Noorderstraat 11 🕑 noon-11pm Mon-Fri, 5-11pm Sat & Sun ♿ fair ♨

Pygma-Lion (4, D1)
South African €€€
One of Amsterdam's most stylish restaurants, Pygma-Lion is an amazing slice of South Africa. However, there is one caveat: if the notion of delicious slices of Bambi (antelope *carpaccio*) and pieces of adorable zebra (meatballs) make you cringe, this one's not for you.

☎ 420 70 22 ✉ Nieuwe Spiegelstraat 5 🕑 11am-10pm Tue-Sat ♿ excellent ♨

Segugio (4, E2)
Italian €€€
This refined little Italian job on busy Utrechtsestraat is one of Amsterdam's best Italian eateries. Well-spaced tables and accomplished handling of first-rate ingredients (such as truffles and scallops) mark it as one for a romantic tête-à-tête, so try not to fill up too much on their excellent risotto.

☎ 330 15 03 ✉ Utrechtsestraat 96 🕑 6-11pm Mon-Sat ♿ good Ⓥ

Silex (4, E2)
French €€€
Just off Utrechtsestraat's eat street area, Silex stands apart with its wide open façade and lack of tourists tucking into its fine-tuned food. It's an intimate split-level restaurant with a creative menu of Mediterranean-influenced French cuisine and an excellent wine list – neither of which disappoints.

☎ 620 59 59 ✉ Kerkstraat 377 🕑 6-10pm Tue-Sat ♿ fair

Take Thai (4, E2)
Thai €€
One of our favourite Thai temples in Amsterdam, its cool, white-on-white décor is at odds with the red-hot food the kitchen serves up. There is a fine starter platter that will have you fighting over portions, and we love the especially authentic massaman curry.

☎ 622 05 77 ✉ Utrechtsestraat 87 🕑 6-10.30pm ♿ excellent ♨ Ⓥ

Take Thai: minimal décor, maximum spice

VEG OUT

While Amsterdammers love their meat, vegetarians are well catered for with most menus featuring at least a couple of meat-free options. There are also several specialist vegetarian restaurants:

- De Bolhoed (p66)
- De Waaghals (p72)
- Green Planet (p63)

Tempo Doeloe (4, E2)
Indonesian €€€

Everyone's favourite Indonesian restaurant in the city is popular with good reason. The classic dishes here are a delight, however, pay attention to the heat level and the friendly waiter's advice – 'no mercy' means just that! Desserts are also delectable. ☎ 625 67 18 ⊠ Utrechtsestraat 75 🕑 6-11.30pm ♿ good ♨ Ⓥ

Vooges (4, E2)
Bistro €€

This casual brown café encourages diners to just rock up and relax over a drink while waiting for a table (there are no bookings after 7pm). The informal menu has a few surprises (such as sweetbreads) but it's workmanlike, filling stuff that's accompanied by a head-bopping, classic pop-rock soundtrack.

☎ 622 05 77 ⊠ Utrechtsestraat 51 🕑 5.30-10.30pm ♨

Wok to Walk (4, C1)
Asian €

Fast food joints in Amsterdam assume that you're either too drunk or stoned to care about what you're eating. However, Wok to Walk serves fast food fresh. Choose noodles or rice, meat or veg, and a sauce. Add to a wok and stir. Brilliant. Other branches at Reguliersbreestraat 45 (2, C8), Kolksteeg 8 (2, C3) and Warmoesstraat 85 (2, D4). ☎ 624 29 41 ⊠ Leidsestraat 96 🕑 9am-late ♿ excellent Ⓥ

Zushi (2, C8)
Japanese €€

This classic conveyor-belt sushi stop appears at first to be nothing out of the ordinary, with its colour-coded plates (to indicate price) and anodyne atmosphere, and while the sushi and sashimi are just ok, we love the delicious soups, flavourful grills, non-smoking policy and decent opening hours. ☎ 330 68 82 ⊠ Amstel 20 🕑 noon-11pm Ⓥ

JODENBUURT, PLANTAGE & THE WATERFRONT

Eenvistweevis (5, B4)
Seafood €€

This unassuming little local favourite located on the Schippersgracht is famous for its short, handwritten menu of whatever is fresh from the sea. While the service is slow and the restaurant gets noisy, it's all about the great oysters, soup and simply prepared mains, such as sole in butter. ☎ 623 28 94 ⊠ Schippersgracht 6 🕑 6-10pm Tue-Sun ♿ good

Plancius (5, B5)
Café €-€€

Right across from Artis Zoo (p22), this stylish brunch/lunch/dinner spot is a welcome alternative to the 'sandwich-only' sadness that plagues most cafés in Amsterdam. Besides having hearty pastas and excellent desserts, any place that does a decent *huevos rancheros* (Mexican ranch eggs) is fine by us. ☎ 330 94 69 ⊠ Plantage Kerklaan 61 🕑 10am-midnight ♿ good ♨ Ⓥ

WORTH A TRIP

Café-Restaurant Amsterdam (1, C2)
French €€€

Housed in a fantastic former water-pumping station with

30m-high ceilings, this modish eatery is one of Amsterdam's best spaces. While it's a little off the tourist trail, the French brasserie classics on offer (think steak tartare, lamb sweetbreads) and the decent wine list make it worth the trip.
☎ 682 26 66 ✉ Watertorenplein 6 ⏱ 11am-1am, to 2am Fri & Sat Ⓥ

Ciel Bleu (4, D6)
French €€€€
Hotel Okura now has a well-earned pair of Michelin-starred restaurants in Ciel Bleu and Yamazato (right). Fantastic views of Amsterdam, matched with sophisticated seasonal fare (several set menus and à la carte), and an extensive wine list, make Ciel Bleu a special Amsterdam eatery.
☎ 678 74 50 ✉ Hotel Okura Amsterdam, Ferdinand Bolstraat 333 ⏱ 6.30-10.30pm Ⓥ

De Kas (1, E4)
International €€€
The idea is simple really. Take some very talented chefs, a herb garden, add a glass greenhouse for a restaurant and open the doors. While it might seem gimmicky, the pure flavours, innovative (but fixed) menu and unique ambiance make this something special. Foodies should opt for the 'chef's table'.
☎ 462 45 62 ✉ Kamerlingh Onneslaan 3, Frankendael Park ⏱ noon-2pm Mon-Fri, 6.30-10pm Mon-Sat ♿ fair Ⓥ

Yamazato (4, D6)
Japanese €€€€
This Michelin-starred restaurant is the one-word answer to the question 'where can you find 'real' Japanese food in Amsterdam?' While Amsterdammers are quick to point out how expensive it is, this is one restaurant in town where it's money well spent. It's a Zen experience, with kimonos, fountains and fabulous sushi.
☎ 678 71 11 ✉ Hotel Okura Amsterdam, Ferdinand Bolstraat 333 ⏱ noon-2pm & 6-9.30pm ♿ fair Ⓥ

Order steak tartare if you dare at Café-Restaurant Amsterdam

Entertainment

Amsterdam's entertainment scene is refreshing. It may not be as so-phisticated as some European cities – minimalist lounge bars and luxe nightclubs are still a new concept to the city, and then, no matter how stylish they are, they don't always work. Amsterdammers don't feel the need to gravitate toward the latest grooviest place – spending quality time outdoors with their friends is what's important. So what makes Amsterdam so enjoyable as a city is that it doesn't feel like a contemporary city – it feels like a cosmopolitan village where everybody knows one another. And some of the best fun to be had is old-fashioned – sharing bottles of wine with friends on a lazy summer afternoon at casual canalside eateries, downing beers in centuries-old cigarette-stained brown cafés, or listening to jazz musicians in dark smoky pubs. It's all so *gezellig*.

Gezelligheid is to be found in places that are cosy and convivial, that are conducive to having a good time – brown cafés, intimate pubs, sunny terraces – places where people can relax, where conversation is easy. It's all to do with companionship and togetherness.

Amsterdam still has plenty of big concert halls, theatres, cinemas and rock venues. Its generous government funding has supported a flourish-ing arts scene with world-renowned orchestras, and ballet and opera companies. Cinemas screen the latest blockbusters and art-house theatres show independent films in their original language. The city hosts festivals and sporting events year round, but really comes alive during summer when there's open-air entertainment in parks, streets and on canals.

Ticket prices are reasonable, although they can be hard to get. Most tickets are available from **Amsterdam Uit Buro** (☎ 0900-01 91; www.aub.nl; cnr Leidseplein & Marnixstraat) or the **Postbank ticket service** (☎ 0900-30 01 25; per min €0.40), music stores, or direct from the venue.

WHAT'S ON IN AMSTERDAM

To find out what's happening, check out the excellent official tourism website, www.iamsterdam.com. The Amsterdam Uit Buro has event information online (www.aub.nl). Depending on your interests, check the sites of clubs and music venues before you leave home, in case you have to get tickets in advance.

When you arrive, pick up free copies of the English-language *Amsterdam Weekly* and *Boom* from bookshops, pubs, cafés, bars and boutiques – most of these places will also have racks with free postcards and leaflets promoting events, concerts, dance parties and club nights.

SPECIAL EVENTS

March

Amsterdam Blues Festival (www .meervaart.nl) The Meervaart Theatre's acclaimed blues festival.

April

Koninginnedag (www.holland.com) Queen's Day hits Amsterdam with a bang on April 30 (sometimes celebrated on the last weekend of the month). More than a million revellers pour into the city to wish Queen Beatrix a happy birthday with lots of drinking, loud music and good cheer. Families head to Vondelpark, while gays and lesbians celebrate on Reguliersdwarsstraat (p97). Everyone else parties anywhere and everywhere.

May

National Windmill Day (www.amsterdam .info/windmills) Windmills are open to the public on the second Saturday in May.

World Press Photo Exhibition (www .worldpressphoto.nl) The world's best international photojournalism competition, held at the Oude Kerk (p27) from May to June.

Vondelpark Open Air Theatre (www .amsterdam.info/parks/vondelpark) Live music, theatre, dance and kids' programmes starting in May and extending throughout the summer.

June-August (summer)

Open Garden Days (www.canalmuseums .nl) View beautiful gardens hidden behind canal houses for three days in June.

Holland Festival (www.hollandfestival.nl) The country's biggest music, drama and dance extravaganza lasts all month and includes everything from highbrow world premieres to one-off fringe events.

Over het IJ Festival (www.overhetij.nl) Exciting performing-arts festival (dance, theatre, music) held at the former NDSM shipyards north of the IJ, from June through August.

North Sea Jazz Festival (www.northseajazz .nl) World's largest jazz festival (p91).

Amsterdam Pride (www.amsterdampride .nl) The city's premier gay and lesbian festival and the world's only gay float parade on water! Held for three days starting the first weekend in August.

Uitmarkt Free previews by local orchestras and theatre and dance troupes.

September

Flower Parade (www.amsterdam.info/ events) A spectacular procession of floats wends its way through the city the first Saturday in September.

Jordaan Festival (www.amsterdam .info/events) A street festival with much merriment and entertainment during the second week of the month.

October-November

Crossing Border (www.crossingborder.nl) A huge literary and music festival held for a month around the Leidseplein attracting interesting and diverse guests.

Sinterklaas Parade (www.stnicholascenter .org) The Christmas season is launched in late November when the Dutch Santa Claus arrives by steamboat and distributes sweets to kids.

Cannabis Cup (www.cannibiscup.com) The marijuana festival is held in the third week of November with awards for the best grass and the biggest spliff.

December

Sinterklaas (www.stnicholascenter.org) St Nicholas Day is 6 December, but gift giving in honour of St Nicholas takes place the evening before on 5 December.

Christmas Day & Boxing Day These popular events are still celebrated on 25 and 26 December.

BARS & CAFÉS

Most bars and cafés serve food during the day, from toasted sandwiches to Asian tapas. Kitchens usually close around 10pm, after which it's next to impossible to even get a packet of crisps.

Centrum

Bar Bep (2, B5)

This casual bar gets crowded with arty locals and students in the afternoon in summer (private parties are often held on the front terrace) and later in the evening when the weather cools down.
☎ 626 56 49 ⌧ Nieuwezijds Voorburgwal 260 ⏲ 4.30pm-1am Mon-Thu, 4.30pm-3am Fri, 11am-3am Sat, 11am-1am Sun ♿ excellent

Blincker (2, C6)

The high ceiling, cosy mezzanine, and mellow atmosphere make Blincker a popular theatre café. At the rear of the Frascati Theatre, it gets crammed with a young student crowd having a pre-theatre meal or post-theatre drinks.

Café de Jaren: gracious and spacious

☎ 627 19 38 ⌨ www .nestheaters.nl ⌧ Sint Barberenstraat 7-9 ⏲ 4pm-1am, 4pm-3am Fri & Sat ♿ good

Bubbles & Wines Champagne Bar (2, C5)

Ignore the silly name, this stylish wine bar is a first for Amsterdam: 54 quality wines by the glass, tasting flights (several different wines to try) and the city's most scrumptious bar food: caviar blinis, cheese plates and our favourite, 'bee stings' – parmesan drizzled with white truffle-infused honey.
☎ 422 33 18 ⌧ Nes 37 ⏲ 3.30pm-1am Mon-Sat ♿ good

Café de Doelen (2, D7)

Dating back to 1895, this atmospheric traditional café with stained glass lamps, carved wooden goat's head, sawdust on the floor inside, and pleasant sun terrace outside, is one of our favourites – so relaxed they don't open on Sundays.
☎ 624 90 23 ⌧ Kloveniersburgwal 125 ⏲ 8am-1am Mon-Thu, to 2am Fri & Sat ♿ good

Café de Jaren (2, C7)

Boasting the most popular terrace in Amsterdam, Café de Jaren is an integral part of the city's bar and café scene. The atmosphere of this huge

---

A BAR BY ANY OTHER NAME

- Brown cafés – stained by centuries of cigarette smoke, with sawdust or sand on the floor.
- Grand cafés – bright and breezy, calm and casual, often elegant and always atmospheric.
- Beer cafés – the focus is on the drinking, pure and simple.
- *Eetcafes* – sandwiches for lunch with your drinks – nothing more, nothing less.
- Theatre cafés – bars attached to theatres, frequented by flamboyant thespians and theatregoers.
- Lounge bars – contemporary in design with comfy sofas, funky sounds and good wines by the glass.
- Coffeeshops – Rastafarian/hippy/boho in style with a chilled-out vibe. Some may sell alcohol, they all make coffee, but their speciality is cannabis.

café is compelling, there's a good selection of drinks and if you get peckish, the food is good (see p63).
☎ 625 57 71 ✉ Nieuwe Doelenstraat 20 ☽ 10am-1am ♿ good

Café De Kroon (4, E1)
Popular with visiting celebrities, this slick place is contemporary in style despite a nod to its heritage (it opened in 1898, although was closed for 50 years) – high ceilings, chandeliers, velvet sofas and a butterfly collection on the walls. It's perfect for cocktails before Escape (p88).
☎ 625 20 11 ✉ Rembrandtplein 17 ☽ noon-1am Sun-Thu, noon-3am Fri & Sat ♿ poor

Café het Schuim (2, B5)
Schuim means 'foam' (on beer) and this grungy, arty bar is extraordinarily popular with beer-swilling locals – it gets packed at any time of the day or night. While the people-watching

can be distracting, it's wise to keep one eye on your belongings.
☎ 638 93 57 ✉ Spuistraat 189 ☽ 11am-1am Mon-Thu, 11am-3am Fri & Sat, 1pm-1am Sun ♿ good

Dantzig (2, E7)
Located on the edge of the Stopera (p94), Dantzig is inundated with thespians and theatregoers looking for a quiet bite (stick to the snacks). Relaxing on the expansive riverside terrace with its beautiful views over the Amstel is a must.
☎ 620 90 39 ✉ Zwanenburgwal 15 ☽ 9am-1am Mon-Thu, 9am-2am Fri & Sat, 10am-11pm Sun ♿ good

De Buurvrouw (2, C6)
This grungy late-night bar is where you inevitably end up when there's nowhere else to go. Take it easy because someone's watching: above the entrance is a bust of *de Buurvrouw* (the woman next door). And yes, everyone *is*

probably as drunk as you. FEBO (p65) anyone?
☎ 625 96 54 ✉ Sint Pieterspoortsteeg 29 ☽ 9pm-3am Mon-Thu, 9pm-4am Fri & Sat ♿ good

Diep (2, B5)
The disco ball, chandeliers and chocolate interior at this otherwise laid-back bar give it a kitsch-camp feel. While it's low-key early in the evening, it gets crowded late with cool young locals when the DJ does his thing.
☎ 420 20 20 ✉ Nieuwezijds Voorburgwal 256 ☽ 5pm-1am Mon-Thu, 5pm-3am Fri & Sat ♿ excellent

Hoppe (2, A7)
Boasting of the city's highest beer turnover, this busy brown café has been in the business since 1670. Once popular with Amsterdam's alternative set, these days its cosy interior, with recycled church pews and beer barrels, tends to attract more camera-wielding tourists than locals.

Hop into Hoppe brown café

☎ 420 44 20 ✉ Spui 18
🕐 8am-1am Mon-Thu,
8am-2am Fri & Sat ♿ good

In't Aepjen (2, E3)

In't Aepjen (literally, 'in the monkeys') is situated in Amsterdam's oldest wooden building (constructed in the 1550s). The bar was named after the pet monkeys that sailors brought back from the tropics – when the sailors ran up too high a bill, the accommodating innkeeper would happily accept primate payments. No, we don't have a euro-monkey currency converter...
☎ 626 84 01 ✉ Zeedijk
1 🕐 3pm-1am Mon-Thu,
3pm-3am Fri & Sat ♿ good

Lime (2, E4)

Thanks to the laid-back contemporary lounge design, funky sounds, fabulous cocktails and friendly staff, this cool bar in Amsterdam's Chinatown (look for the Buddhist temple) is by far the best in this sleazy part of the city.
☎ 639 30 20 ✉ Zeedijk
104 🕐 5pm-1am Mon-Thu

AMSTERDAM'S BEST BARS
- In't Aepjen (left)
- Van Puffelen (p84)
- Café van Zuylen (opposite)
- Café de Jaren (p80)
- Weber (p86)
- Lime (left)
- Wolvenstraat 23 (p84)
- Bubbles & Wines Champagne Bar (p80)

& Sun, 5pm-3am Fri & Sat ♿ excellent

Lokaal 't Loosje (2, E5)

Popular with British tourists on beer-drinking tours and bucks nights, this brown café, one of the area's oldest, has an atmospheric interior with gorgeous tiles on the walls, although most miss it because they can't get past the sun terrace.
☎ 627 26 35 ✉ Nieuwmarkt 32-34 🕐 9.30am-1am, 9.30am-3am Fri & Sat ♿ good

Luxembourg (2, A7)

This once-elegant grand café has seen better days, although its faded charm

still makes it undeniably atmospheric. These days it's over-run with tourists who enjoy people-watching from the sun terrace. If you prefer to hang out with the locals, head inside for a drink.
☎ 620 62 64 ✉ Spui 22-24 🕐 9am-1am Sun-Thu, 9am-2am Fri & Sat ♿ good

Jordaan

Blender (1, C2)

This super-slick bar-restaurant-club boasts an enormous curved bar, colourful décor, Eames chairs and rainbow-lit restrooms. Due to its location west of the Western Canal Belt, it's way off the bucks/hens tourist trail – so make the effort

Luxembourg: lounge with locals

Café de Pels: home to tradition and drinkers' ambition

to get here and see where Amsterdam's grooviest set hang out.

☎ 486 98 60 ⊠ Van der Palmkade 16 ⏰ 6pm-1am Tue-Sun ♿ fair

Café Thijssen (2, A1)
The Art Deco-influenced interior of this laid-back bar is part of the attraction for the undeniably local crowd of regular drinkers. Visitors to the city call in because they want just that – a truly unpretentious 'local' experience.

☎ 623 89 94 ⊠ Brouwersgracht 107 ⏰ 11am-1am Sun-Thu, 11am-3am Fri & Sat ♿ good

Finch (2, A1)
This funky lounge-bar, which belongs to the Wolvenstraat team, attracts a hip crowd of locals and expats to what is both one of the Jordaan's most relaxed and buzzy neighbourhood squares. When equally cool Proust bar next door also gets going, the place just hums.

☎ 626 24 61 ⊠ Noordermarkt 5 ⏰ 9am-1am Sun-Thu, 9am-3am Fri & Sat ♿ good

Het Papeneiland (2, A1)
This 17th-century bar is full of history, with gorgeous blue Delft tiles, an antique stove, and entrance to a (no longer) secret tunnel to a once clandestine church across the canal. It attracts mature locals who pack the place in the evening, so head here early for a drink.

☎ 624 19 89 ⊠ Prinsengracht 2 ⏰ 10am-1am Mon-Thu, 10am-2am Fri & Sat, noon-1am Sun ♿ poor

't Smalle (3, B3)
This beautifully restored former *jenever* (gin) bar and tasting house dates back to 1786. Its interior is worth a look, however it's the gorgeous canalside terrace, especially romantic at night, that attracts most.

☎ 623 96 17 ⊠ Egelantiersgracht 12 ⏰ 10am-1am ♿ good

Western Canal Belt

Café de Pels (3, C6)
The action at this appealingly shabby traditional brown café – attracting a mix of students, academics and creative types – is focused on drinking. It's also a Sunday morning breakfast fave.

☎ 622 90 37 ⊠ Huidenstraat 25 ⏰ 10am-1am (to 2am Fri & Sat) ♿ fair

Café het Molenpad (3, B6)
It's near impossible to snag a canalside table on this lovely stretch of canal, so slide onto the wooden bench under the window of Café het Molenpad, one of the city's most atmospheric old cafés. Their snack plates are super for sharing with friends.

☎ 625 96 80 ⊠ Prinsenstraat 653 ⏰ noon-1am Mon-Thu & Sun, noon-2am Fri & Sat ♿ fair

Café van Zuylen (2, B4)
Although the sun terrace is one of the prettiest spots for a drink on the Singel, the

TWO FINGERS OF FROTH
Those toasting their first beer on Dutch soil are often disappointed by the two-finger-deep head of froth on their (cold) beers. Apart from trapping in the flavour, it's actually a good indicator of whether or not the beer has been watered down – if it has, the head sinks quickly, otherwise it stays foamy for up to five minutes.

interior – with its cosy rooms featuring lots of wood and old leather banquettes – is just as appealing in the cooler months.
☎ 639 10 55 ✉ Torensteeg 4 🕑 10am-1am Sun-Thu, 10am-3am Fri & Sat 🚻 good

De Doffer (3, B6)
Local sales staff from the Nine Streets shops love lunching at this laid-back brown café. Just as the shopping bag-laden tourists like to sit in the sun to rest their weary legs. The club sandwiches go well with their cold beers. It's just as popular on balmy summer evenings.
☎ 622 66 86 ✉ Runstraat 12-14 🕑 10am-1am Sun-Thu, 10am-3am Fri & Sat 🚻 good

De Pieper (4, B1)
Our local favourite is one of Amsterdam's oldest (1665) and most authentic brown cafés – stained-glass windows, sand on the floor, good-humoured service and a cuddly black-and-white cat is what makes it so likeable. The outside terrace, overlooking one of Prinsengracht's prettiest parts, is an added bonus.
☎ 626 47 75 ✉ Prinsengracht 424 🕑 11am-1am Mon-Thu, 11am-3am Fri & Sat 🚻 fair

De Vergulde Gaper (2, A2)
The 'gaper' above the awning is one of the few signs left that this atmospheric old-fashioned bar – popular with locals – was once a pharmacy. No matter, a seat on the terrace with a glass of white wine is as medicinal as anything that might have once been on this shop's shelves.
☎ 624 89 75 ✉ Prinsenstraat 30 🕑 10am-1am Sun-Thu, 10am-3am Fri & Sat 🚻 fair

G-Spot (4, B1)
Next door to De Pieper (left), this contemporary minimalist bar-restaurant with its bright light-filled interior couldn't be more different to its brown café neighbour, but it's equally as appealing. While the interior is stylish, the canalside terrace with pretty views will keep you outside. Good wines by the glass.

☎ 320 37 33 ✉ Prinsengracht 422 🕑 11am-1am 🚻 fair

Van Puffelen (3, B5)
It's difficult to get a table on the terrace outside, but we never care because we love the wooden interior of this big brown café and the laid-back attitude of the locals we meet. The drinks are some of Amsterdam's cheapest and the croquettes are delicious.
☎ 624 62 70 ✉ Prinsengracht 377 🕑 3pm-1am Mon-Thu, noon-2am Fri & Sat, noon-1am Sun 🚻 good

Werck (3, B4)
While the wonderful food here deserves a try (p71) this is also a popular bar. Tourists needing a drink after visiting the sobering Anne Frank Huis (p10), next door, like to imbibe on the terrace, while locals like the rooftop on balmy summer evenings. Inside, a DJ gets people grooving.
☎ 627 40 79 ✉ Prinsengracht 277 🕑 10am-1am Mon-Thu, 10am-3am Fri-Sat

Wolvenstraat 23 (3, C5)
This funky bar with no name (we challenge you to find a sign anywhere) is especially

Keep the wolf from the door at Wolvenstraat

popular with locals, who come for the good wines by the glass, great music and tasty Asian snacks. If this is your kind of place, also check out their other bar, Finch (p83).

☎ 320 08 43 ✉ Wolven-straat 23 🕑 9am-1am Sun-Thu, 9am-3am Fri & Sat ♿ good

Southern Canal Belt

Cafe Americaan (4, B2)
The Art Deco interior of this grand café, with its vaulted ceiling and stained-glass windows, is one of Amsterdam's most stylish and easily justifies a drink or two here to have a peek.

☎ 556 32 32 ✉ Leid-sekade 97 🕑 7am-10pm ♿ good

De Balie (4, B2)
While this café is attached to Amsterdam's most active cultural/intellectual centre (of the same name) – and occasionally sees lively political debate take place after documentary screenings – these days it tends to mainly attract tourists because it's so close to the Leidseplein.

☎ 553 51 30 ✉ Kleine Gartmanplantsoen 10 🕑 10am-1am Mon-Thu, 10am-2am Fri & Sat ♿ poor

De Smoeshaan (4, B2)
Laid-back during the day, this theatre-café gets lively before and after perform-ances. It's a good drinking spot if you're staying in the area and are fed up with the masses of tourists around Leidseplein.

☎ 625 03 68 ✉ Leid-sekade 90 🕑 11am-1am, Sun-Thu, 11am-2am Fri & Sat ♿ poor

Kamer 401 (4, B1)
This glamorous bar glows at night, as do the gorgeous-looking cocktail-drinking young locals who pack the place till late. With DJs pro-viding a funky soundtrack, it's perfect for pre-clubbing drinks.

☎ 422 44 53 ✉ Marnix-straat 401 🕑 4pm-1am Sun-Thu, 4pm-3am Fri & Sat ♿ poor

Janvier (4, E2)
There's no lovelier place to sit on a sunny afternoon than under the shade of the plane trees at this stylish bar-restaurant. Stick to a drink

and snacks (the food can be hit and miss) and watch the kids kick a football around in this pleasant down-to-earth neighbourhood.

☎ 626 11 99 ✉ Amstel-veld 12 🕑 noon-midnight ♿ fair

Lux (4, B1)
One of several happen-ing bars along this street, attracting beautiful young Amsterdammers and expats-in-the-know. Good DJs keep the crowds happy and the bar staff very, very busy.

☎ 422 14 12 ✉ Marnix-straat 403 🕑 8pm-3am Sun-Thu, 8pm-4am Fri & Sat ♿ poor

Oosterling (4, E2)
Operating since the 18th century, and by the same

Cafe Americaan: the oldest and most stylish of Amsterdam's grand cafés

DRINKING JENEVER – A PRIMER

Jenever (Dutch gin) is made from juniper berries and drunk chilled from thimble-size glasses. Most prefer smooth *jonge* (young) *jenever*. *Oude* (old) *jenever* has a strong juniper flavour and is an acquired taste. A *kopstoot* (head butt) is a glass of *jenever* with a beer chaser. More than a few *kopstoot* will definitely lead to a *hoofdpijn* (headache). You can try *jenevers* and liqueurs at *proeflokalen* (tasting houses), once attached to distilleries – a hangover from the 17th century when scores operated in Amsterdam.

family since the 19th century, Oosterling was once a tea and coffee distribution outlet for the United East Indian Company. It's popular with locals who pack the place after work.
☎ 623 41 40 ✉ Utrechtsestraat 140 ☼ noon-1am Sun-Thu, noon-3am Fri & Sat ♿ good

Suzie Wong (4, B1)
Like a cross between a Wong Kar Wai movie set and a kitsch Asian lounge bar, Suzie Wong's attracts a crowd that changes like the wind – one night beautiful locals sip cocktails before heading to Jimmy Woo's (p88), another night rowdy guys/girls on a bucks/hens night are doing shots.
☎ 626 67 69 ✉ Korte Leidsedwarsstraat 45 ☼ 8pm-3am (to 4am Fri & Sat) ♿ poor

Weber (4, B1)
We love this buzzy bar for its loud indie music, retro décor and unpretentious local vibe. Cheap drinks and friendly service are an added incentive to head here on a Saturday night – if you can squeeze in!
☎ 627 05 74 ✉ Marnixstraat 397 ☼ 8pm-3am Mon-Thu, 8pm-4am Fri-Sun ♿ poor

De Pijp
Café de Pijp (4, D4)
This funky café is very contemporary in style with fabulous lighting and chilled-out sounds. Although when the place fills with cool young locals on weekends, you can't hear the music above the chatter.
☎ 670 41 61 ✉ Ferdinand Bolstraat 17-19 ☼ 3pm-1am Mon-Fri, noon-1am Sat & Sun (to 3am Fri & Sat) ♿ good

Chocolate (4, D4)
On a great little pedestrian street with several bars that get crowded with locals on summer evenings, this groovy lounge bar is the standout. While Chocolate's terrace is the most popular, we love the vibe inside.
☎ 675 76 72 ✉ 1e van der Helststraat 62a ☼ 10am-1am Sun-Thu, 10am-3am Fri & Sat ♿ fair

Kingfisher (4, D4)
Kingfisher's casual brand of cool and laid-back bar staff ensure it's always crammed with locals (lots of students) out to have a good time and catch up with friends – it's the kind of place that quickly becomes your 'local'.
☎ 671 23 95 ✉ Ferdinand Bolstraat 24 ☼ 11am-1am Mon-Thu, 11am-3am Fri & Sat ♿ good

The Mansion (4, B2)
While it's best to make a dinner reservation to get through the door, the contemporary Chinese can be hit and miss. We prefer the glam cocktail bars – very luxe. Think chandeliers, baroque chairs, patterned wallpaper and fibre optic lighting. There's also a club, but it's as unpredictable as the restaurant.
☎ 616 66 64 ✉ Hobbemastraat 2 ☼ 6pm-1am Tue-Thu & Sun, 6pm-3am Fri & Sat

Dive in for a good time at the Kingfisher

Café De Sluyswacht: not a bad place for a lock-in

Jodenbuurt, Plantage & the Islands

Bierbrouwerij 't IJ (5, E6)
Locals love nothing more than sitting outside on a summer's evening drinking beer at this brewery in the shadow of the De Gooyer windmill (p29). Trams 9 and 14 will get you there.
☎ 622 83 25 ✉ Funenkade 7 ⏲ 3-8pm Wed-Sun ♿ good

De Sluyswacht (2, E6)
This brown café in a former lock-keeper's house leans heavily to one side.But the building has been here since 1695, so it's not going anywhere fast. A drink on the terrace on a sunny afternoon is sublime.
☎ 330 94 63 ✉ Jodenbre-estraat 1 ⏲ 11.30am-1am Mon-Thu, 11.30am-3am Fri & Sat, 11.30am-7pm Sun

Odessa (1, F3)
Not as hip as it was when it first opened, this funky Russian boat with bar on deck and disco below is worth visiting if you're staying at the Lloyd (p102) or on your way to Panama (p88), but don't make a special trip.
☎ 419 30 10 ✉ Veemkade 259 ⏲ 6pm-1am Mon, 11am-1am Tue-Sun ♿ poor

Tisfris (2, E6)
Brimming with good cheer, this place is popular with a mix of creative locals, art-school students and shoppers stopping in after rummaging through the stalls at nearby Water-looplein flea market. Its affable staff serve up decent glasses of wine and beer, along with scrumptious salads and sandwiches, on the sunny canalside terrace.
☎ 622 04 72 ✉ Sint Antoniesbreestraat 142 ⏲ 9am-7pm ♿ good

CLUBS

Thursday, Friday and Saturday are the busiest nights for clubbing in Amsterdam, with Sunday not far behind. You'll drink alone before 11pm and all venues close around 4am. Club prices vary from free, if you head there early (but a very un-cool thing to do in Amsterdam when there are plenty of good bars), to €5, for a local DJ, and anywhere up to €30 for a major dance party with a long international DJ line-up. Dress standards are cool but casual, although sneakers aren't accepted in the hippest venues.

Bitterzoet (2, C3)
This offbeat nightspot, close to the budget hotel district and the student quarter, naturally sees a young inter-national crowd pass through its doors for its live music, DJs and alternative theatre. Expect different styles of music on different nights, from grungy indie sounds to global fusion.
☎ 521 30 01 🖥 www .bitterzoet.com ✉ Spuist-raat 2 ⏲ 8pm-3am Mon-Thu & Sun, 8pm-4am Fri & Sat ♿ good

DOOR LIST/DOOR BITCH

Amsterdammers may not dress up as much as clubbers elsewhere, but there's a certain casual chic about their style that you'd be wise to copy to get by the door bitch. Leave the sneakers at home for a start. And groups of guys may have difficulty getting in without girls. One sure way of securing entry is to get on a door list – most people don't realise you can sign up via club websites or by calling ahead to reserve a table. Many clubs charge admission of €5 to €15 depending on the night.

Eleven (5, A3)

On the 11th floor of the old post office building (home to the Stedelijk Museum p14) with spectacular city views, this arty, edgy bar-restaurant-club is one of Amsterdam's hippest spots. A more mature lot start early for sunset drinks, with young clubbers arriving after 11pm for everything from electro to techno.
☎ 573 29 11 ☐ www
.ilove11.nl ✉ Oosterdok-skade 5 ☽ noon-1am
Mon-Wed & Sun, noon-4am
Thu-Sat ☐ excellent

Escape & Escape Delux (2, D8)

Although sexy Escape has existed since the '80s (forever in nightclub years) its different themed nights (Sundae, Franchise, Pure, Luxury, Allure, etc) and new intimate space, Escape Delux, ensure it stays fresh. Clubbers love it and are happy to line up for it – so join the queue.
☎ 622 11 11 ☐ www
.escape.nl ✉ Rembrandt
plein 11 for Escape; Am-stel 70 for Escape Delux
☽ 11pm-4am Thu &
Sun, 11pm-5am Fri & Sat
☐ good

Jimmy Woo (4, B1)

The oriental opium-den décor, exotic vibe and exceptional DJs make it just as difficult to get into Jimmy

Woo now as it was when it first opened. Dress glam, get to know the door staff and get on a list to guarantee yourself entry to what is still Amsterdam's coolest club.
☎ 626 31 50 ☐ www
.jimmywoo.com ✉ Korte
Leidsedwarsstraat 18
☽ 11pm-3am Wed, Thu
& Sun, 11pm-4am Fri & Sat
☐ fair

Melkweg (4, B1)

The Milky Way – it's housed in a former dairy – must be Amsterdam's coolest club-gallery-cinema-café-concert hall. Its vibrant program of events is so full and varied that it's impossible not to find something you want to go to, from international DJ club nights to live Brazilian jazz.
☎ 531 81 81 ☐ www
.melkweg.nl ✉ Lijnbaans-gracht 234a ☽ varies; check
website ☐ excellent

Nomads (3, A5)

This Arabian Supperclub (it's from the same team) is another concept bar-restaurant-club, but with a Middle Eastern vibe. You start off reclining on cushioned lounge beds and feasting on meze, next you're shimmying with a belly dancer, and by the end of the night you're dancing to Arabic fusion sounds. *Ya habibi.*

☎ 344 64 01 ☐ www
.restaurantnomads.nl ✉ Ro-zengracht 133 ☽ 8pm-3am
(to 4am Fri & Sat) ☐ good

Odeon (2, A7)

In 2005, a glam make-over to this grand canal house created several separate stylish spaces, including an uber-cool bar with themed nights (we love *Paradise* and *Passion*), a sumptuous bar with Singel views, a dramatic-looking restaurant, and a funky basement brasserie serving delicious snacks and meals (11am to 1am daily).
☎ 521 85 55 ☐ www
.odeonamsterdam.nl ✉ Sin-gel 460 ☽ club 11pm-4am
Thu-Sat; bar 6pm-1am Wed,
6pm-4am Thu-Sun ☐ good

Panama (1, E3)

A full schedule of themed nights and international DJs, from Deep Dish to DJ Tiesto, sees Panama's club packed most nights. You'll get everything from house to Latin fusion, along with live music and comedy. Despite having a Central American name the décor is Asian – but who cares, the cocktails are great.
☎ 311 86 86 ☐ www
.panama.nl ✉ Oostelijke
Handelskade 4 ☽ daily,
times vary depending on night. Check website.

Paradiso (4, C2)

Amsterdam's best live-music venue becomes a club when the bands finish, usually around midnight. Expect interesting dance music, anything from Finnish DJs spinning jazz to Afro New Wave from New York and tech-hop from Detroit. ☎ 626 45 21 ⌨ www .paradiso.nl ✉ Weteringschans 6 🕑 Fri-Sun 11.30pm-4am ♿ poor

Rain (2, D8)

From the moody décor to the mix of music – from chill-out lounge to global fusions and funk and soul – a night out at this sultry, stylish bar-restaurant-club is an assault on the senses. ☎ 626 70 78 ⌨ www .rain-amsterdam.com ✉ Rembrandtplein 44 🕑 8pm-3am (to 4am Fri & Sat) ♿ good

Sugar Factory (4, B1)

In a super location next to Melkweg (opposite), behind cool bar Weber (p86) and with Jimmy Woo (opposite) a block away, you can have a big night without leaving the 'hood. Sugar Factory does everything – hip-hop, house, drum'n'bass, soul, funk, electronica, pop and disco – and does it well. ☎ 626 50 06 ⌨ www .sugarfactory.nl ✉ Lijnbaansgracht 238 🕑 6.30pm-1am Mon-Thu, 6.30pm-2am Fri & Sat, 7pm-1am Sun ♿ good

To Night (1, E4)

Hotel Arena's club hosts radically different nights from one night to the next, with top international DJ line-ups and special one-off parties. Whatever the style of music it's worth a look just to see the cool interior of this former chapel. ☎ 694 74 44 ⌨ www .hotelarena.nl ✉ 's-Gravesandestraat 51 🕑 10pm-3am Thu & Sun, to 4am Fri & Sat ♿ good

Vakzuid (1, B5)

This super-stylish bar-club-restaurant attracts an older glamorous set to its different club nights – disco is popular and *Lovebeats* especially so. During the day the gorgeous bar-restaurant is open for lunch. ☎ 521 30 01 ⌨ www .vakzuid.nl ✉ Olympic Stadium 🕑 10am-1am Sun-Thu, 10am-3am Fri & Sat ♿ good

Winston International (2, D4)

This grungy venue can get pretty wild depending on the night – expect anything from hip-hop to house but most of all expect the unexpected. Check their website for agenda details. ☎ 623 13 80 ⌨ www .winston.nl ✉ Warmoesstraat 129 🕑 10pm-3am Sun-Thu, 10pm-4am Fri & Sat ♿ good

CINEMAS

Amsterdam always seems to have an excellent selection of art-house and independent films showing. With the exception of

In ecstasy at Paradiso

children's films, movies are screened in their original language with Dutch subtitles. Dutch-language films have *Nederlands Gesproken* after the title.

Filmmuseum (4, A2)
The museum owns more than 40,000 films and regularly screens everything from silent classics to contemporary Iranian art house in its beautiful Vondelpark pavilion. Films are also shown outdoors on the beautiful terrace during summer, but get there early to get a seat.
☎ 589 14 00 ☐ www .filmmuseum.nl ☐ Vondelpark 3 ☺ €2.50-€11 depending on film event ♿ good

Kriterion (1, E4)
The much-loved Kriterion shows a vibrant mix of cult, classic and indie flicks. Recent programmes have included a Hitchcock retrospective and director-driven classics from the '70s such as Scorsese's *Taxi Driver*.
☎ 623 17 08 ☐ www .kriterion.nl ☐ Roetersstraat 170 € €7.50/6 ☺ 10am-late ♿ good

Melkweg (4, B1)
Melkweg (p88) has a cool little cinema showing a discerning selection of films from art-house to world cinema. Its 'cult corner' screenings are worth looking out for.
☎ 531 81 81 ☐ Lijnbaansgracht 234a € €6/4 ♿ excellent

Movies (3, B1)
The four screens here exhibit a mixed bag of the

Mov(i)e along to the Tuschinskitheater

better mainstream films, kitsch cult cinema, avant-garde Euro flicks and rarely screened gems. A meal in the Wild Kitchen, the gorgeous Art Deco restaurant attached to the cinema, is a perfect prelude to an intermission-free film.
☎ 638 60 16 ☐ www .themovies.nl ☐ Haarlemmerdijk 161 € adult/student/child €8/7/6.50 ☺ 1.30pm-midnight ♿ good

Pathé Cinemas (4, D1)
The two adjacent Pathé theatres share the same box office and while both screen mainstream blockbusters, they also show some art-house and indie cinema.
☎ 0900-14 58 (per min €0.40) ☐ www.pathe.nl

☐ Vijzelstraat 14 € €6-9 ☺ 11am-midnight ♿ excellent

Tuschinskitheater (2, C8)
Amsterdam's most beautiful cinema, this Art Deco picture palace is worth a visit just to see its splendid interior. The main theatre shows commercial cinema and the smaller one offers art house and indie.
☎ 626 26 33 ☐ www .pathe.nl ☐ Reguliersbreestraat 26 € €8-10 ☺ noon-10pm ♿ poor

ROCK, JAZZ & BLUES

Akhnaton (2, C3)
An excellent place to hear world music and global dance beats – everything

from African rhythms and Brazilian bossa nova to Arabic fusion and Persian pop.
☎ 624 33 96
🖥 www.akhnaton.nl
✉ Nieuwezijds Kolk 25
€ varies 🕙 11pm–5am Fri & Sat 🚹 poor

Alto Jazz Cafe (4, C2)
A renowned live jazz venue in the touristy Leidseplein area, this small smoky venue is nevertheless the place where serious jazz fans go to hear everything from improvisational jazz to classic blues.
☎ 626 32 49 ✉ Korte Leidsedwarsstraat 115
€ free 🕙 9pm–3am Mon-Thu & Sun, 9pm–4am Fri & Sat 🚹 good

ArenA Stadium (1, E6)
This enormous stadium is the venue for mega tour-ing shows from Madonna to Robbie Williams, and is also home to the local Ajax football team.
☎ 311 13 33 🖥 www .amsterdamarena.nl
✉ Arena Boulevard 1, Bijlmer € varies 🕙 box office 9am–6pm Ⓜ 54 (in the direction of Gein) 🚹 excellent

Bimhuis (5, B2)
A great space in the stunning Muziekgebouw building in the docklands waterfront area, Bimhuis is Amsterdam's leading jazz venue and sees the best international musicians perform. It's an

interesting 10-minute walk from the station or take trams 4, 9 or 14.
☎ 788 21 88 🖥 www .bimhuis.nl ✉ Piet Heinkade 3, Waterfront area
€ €12-20 🕙 varies, check website 🚹 excellent

Heineken Music Hall (1, E6)
A wide range of interna-tional acts – from the big names in indie music to more mainstream popular bands – perform at this excellent space. Whoever you're seeing, get here early. If you don't want to be in the mosh pit, head upstairs for a seat.
☎ 900 300 1250 🖥 www .heineken-music-hall.nl
✉ ArenA Boulevard 590, Bijlmermeer € varies
🕙 box office 9am–6pm
Ⓜ 54 (in the direction of Gein) 🚹 excellent

Maloe Melo (3, A5)
Home to Amsterdam's blues scene, this rather dingy venue

Brassed off at Bimhuis

has a full roster of local and international blues musicians. While you're there, check in to see if there's anything interesting on at rock venue Korsakoff (☎ 625 78 54, Lijnbaansgracht 161) next door.

☎ 420 45 92 ✉ Lijnbaansgracht 163 € free ⏰ 9pm-3am Tue-Thu, 9pm-4am Fri-Sun ♿ fair

Melkweg (4, B1)
Melkweg (p88 and p90) has an adventurous live-music program that includes top international acts and local talent performing everything from Latin jazz to world music. Buy tickets from the Melkweg box office, Uit Buro (p78) or music shops.

☎ 624 17 77 🖥 www .melkweg.nl ✉ Lijnbaansgracht 234 € varies ⏰ 7.30pm-4am Sun & Tue-Thu, 7.30pm-5am Fri & Sat ♿ excellent

Paradiso (4, C2)
This grand neo-Gothic church (p89) is the city's best (and legendary) live music venue – anyone and everyone performs here, from Gotan Project to James Brown. Get your tickets well in advance for big names.

☎ 626 45 21 🖥 www .paradiso.nl ✉ Weteringschans 6 € varies ⏰ 8.30pm-midnight ♿ good

Tropentheater (5, D6)
This is the place in Amsterdam to come for the most interesting music, song, dance and theatre from around the globe – from Rwandan drums to Algerian rai.

☎ 568 85 00 🖥 www .tropentheater.nl ✉ Tropen-

TOP FIVE LIVE MUSIC SPACES
- Bimhuis (p91)
- Paradiso (left)
- Melkweg (left)
- Heineken Music Hall (p91)
- Tropentheater (left

museum, Linnaeusstraat 2 € varies ⏰ varies ♿ good

THEATRE & COMEDY

Amsterdam has a variety of venues showing everything from alternative theatre to mainstream musicals. Performances are mainly in Dutch – summer is your best bet for catching shows in English.

Boom Chicago (4, B1)
This hilarious English-language improv troupe has been entertaining locals and tourists for years. If you think you'd like to get involved they even offer improv classes.

☎ 423 01 01 🖥 www .boomchicago.nl ✉ Leidseplein 12 € €10-22 ⏰ box office 11.30am-8.30pm; shows 7.30pm & 10.30pm but can vary, so check ahead. ♿ fair

Felix Meritis (3, B5)
This wonderful arts, cultural and intellectual space (p26) occasionally hosts experimental and emerging European theatre, along with innovative music and dance.

☎ 626 23 21 🖥 www.felixmeritis.nl ✉ Keizersgracht 324 € varies ⏰ box office 10am-5pm Mon-Sat ♿ excellent

Frascati (2, C6)
Young Dutch directors, choreographers and producers get to develop their talents at this experimental theatre venue. While performances are mostly in Dutch, occasionally there are English-language plays, so check ahead.

☎ 626 68 66 🖥 www .nestheaters.nl ✉ Nes 63 € free most of the time ⏰ varies, check website ♿ fair

Koninklijk Theater Carré
(4, F2)

Built in 1887, the grand Koninklijk Theater Carré is Amsterdam's largest theatre (it seats 1700) and hosts everything from blockbuster musicals to acrobatic circuses.

☎ 252 52 55
🖥 www.theatercarre.nl
✉ Amstel 115-125
€ €15-90 ⏲ box office & information 9am-9pm; show times vary ♿ excellent

Stadsschouwburg
(4, B2)

This beautiful baroque building is the city's most impressive theatre, hosting large-scale productions, operas, operettas, classical music concerts, dance and theatre. During summer, English-language performances are scheduled.

☎ 624 23 11
✉ Leidseplein 26 € 12-80
⏲ box office 10am-6pm; show times vary
♿ excellent

Theater Bellevue & Nieuwe de la Mar Theater
(4, B1)

While these two theatre groups merged in the 1980s, they retained their separate identities. The Bellevue does popular theatre (modern, dance, cabaret and musical theatre) with the odd performance in English, while Nieuwe de la Mar stages more experimental, home-grown performances, along with excellent international acts.

☎ 530 53 01 (Bellevue), 530 53 02 (Nieuwe de la Mar)
🖥 www.theaterbellevue.nl, www.nieuwedelamarthea-tre.nl ✉ Leidsekade 90 (Bellevue), Marnixstraat 404 (Nieuwe de la Mar) € varies ⏲ box office 11am-6pm ♿ excellent

CLASSICAL MUSIC, OPERA & DANCE

Concertgebouw (4, B4)

Amsterdam's world-famous concert hall (see p28) has exceptional acoustics, attracting internationally renowned soloists, orchestras and chamber groups. The resident Royal Concertge-bouw Orchestra is one of the world's most esteemed companies.

☎ 573 05 11 (24 hours, in English), 671 83 45
🖥 www.concertgebouw.nl
✉ Concertgebouwplein 2-6
€ varies, last minute tickets cost €7.50 ⏲ box office 10am-8.15pm, performance times vary ♿ good

Muziekgebouw aan't IJ
(5, B2)

This magnificent new building is home to some of the world's best musicians and plays elegant host to everything from philharmonic orchestras to harp festivals.

☎ 788 20 00
🖥 www.muziekgebouw.nl
✉ Piet Heinkade 1
€ €8.50-27.50; you can buy tickets online
⏲ varies, check website
♿ excellent

Head in the clouds: the beautiful façade of the Stadsschouwburg

CHURCH CONCERTS

Wonderful concerts are held several nights a week in the city's beautiful churches. Organ concerts, choral and chamber music can be seen at the **Nieuwe Kerk** (p26; ☎ 638 69 09); the **Oude Kerk** (p18; ☎ 625 82 84); the **Westerkerk** (p31; ☎ 624 77 66), and the **Museum of our Lord in the Attic** (p24; ☎ 624 66 04). Access a programme at www.amsterdamorganconcerts.nl.

Muziektheater (2, E8)

The enormous concert halls of the Muziektheater, or Stopera (p31), boast excellent programs of top local and international ballets and operas, along with modern-dance performances. Book ahead if either of the two resident companies, the Netherlands Opera and the Netherlands National Ballet, is performing.
☎ 625 54 55 🖳 www .hetmuziektheater.nl ✉ Waterlooplein 22 € varies, discounts apply so check website ⌚ box office 10am-6pm Mon-Sat ♿ good

COFFEESHOPS

While coffeeshops in the Netherlands are tolerated (in the typical Dutch spirit of openness) cannabis products are actually illegal. The Dutch police simply turn a blind eye to soft drugs for personal use – you can safely carry up to 5g. Dope can be bought hassle-free in around 250 coffeeshops, but there are a few rules: buy from coffeeshops and never from street dealers, always check that it's okay before lighting up, and go easy on that first smoke because Amsterdam's dope is strong.

Abraxas (2, B5)

This sprawling coffee shop's eclectic décor, friendly staff, internet access and live DJs attract a young international globetrotting set. It's a good place to head if you're a coffeeshop virgin.
☎ 625 57 63 ✉ Jonge Roelensteeg 12 ⌚ 10am-1am ♿ poor

Barney's (2, B1)

Barney's new-age atmosphere, fresh juices and hearty breakfasts (ideal for those with the munchies) have been pulling in punters for years. For many, there's no better way to start the day in Amsterdam.
☎ 625 97 61 ✉ Haarlemmerstraat 102 ⌚ 7am-8pm ♿ poor

Dampring (2, B7)

Before it was made famous by its role in *Ocean's Twelve*, Dampring was already popular with locals and travellers for its organically grown dope, and was consistently awarded the Cannabis Cup for its fine products. Rumour has it that a couple of the movie's stars were regulars long before Dampring's starring appearance.
☎ 625 97 61 ✉ Haarlemmerstraat 102 ⌚ 10am-1am ♿ poor

Greenhouse (2, D5)

Greenhouse's psychedelic vibe and high quality Dutch-grown weed keeps the connoisseurs coming back for more. The Dam central location and the fact that they serve alcohol is an added extra.
☎ 627 17 39 ✉ Oudezijds Voorburgwal 191 ⌚ 9am-1am Mon-Thu & Sun, 9am-3am Fri & Sat ♿ poor

Kadinsky (2, B6)

Those not into the grungy, hippy feel of most Amsterdam coffeeshops love Kadinsky for its clean, contemporary style,

Cure the munchies at Barney's, one of Amsterdam's famous coffeeshops

funky music, friendly service and infamous space cakes. Others, however, feel it's all gone a little corporate.

☎ 624 70 23 ✉ Rosmarijnsteeg 9 ⏰ 10am-1am, Mon-Fri, 10am-2am Sat & Sun

La Tertulia (3, B6)

Run by a delightful mother and daughter team, this laid-back, plant-filled canalside coffeeshop (with a pretty terrace) has a reputation for having the best space cakes in town. They also do delicious juices, herbal teas and *tosti* (toasted sandwiches) when you get the munchies.

☎ 623 85 03 ✉ Prinsengracht 312 ⏰ 11am-7pm Tue-Sat

Rokerij (4, C1)

Rokerij's Eastern décor and candlelight attract those tired with the Rastafarian vibe. Staff have a reputation for friendliness and they also serve alcohol. Rokerij has other branches throughout the city, but this is the flagship branch.

☎ 422 66 43 ✉ Lange Leidsedwarsstraat 41

⏰ 10am-1am Mon-Thu & Sun, 10am-3am Fri & Sat ♿ good

Siberie (2, C2)

This bright, clean coffeeshop – with its regular live jazz sets, DJs, art exhibitions and resident astrologer – is refreshing. It goes without saying that their weed is considered top quality.

☎ 623 59 09 🖳 www .siberie.nl ✉ Brouwersgracht 11 ⏰ 11am-11pm Mon-Thu & Sun, 11am-midnight Fri & Sat ♿ good

GAY & LESBIAN AMSTERDAM

Amsterdam decriminalised homosexuality in the 1800s and celebrated the world's first gay marriage in 2002. The city's gay scene is Europe's most liberal – gay and lesbian venues are everywhere and there's a plethora of weekly queer club nights held at straight clubs. Make your first point of call the **Pink Point** (☎ 428 10 70 🖳 www

.pinkpoint.org ✉ Westermarkt, near Homomonument ⏰ 9am-8pm) where you can pick up the *Gay Map to Amsterdam* (www.gay amsterdam.com) and *Gay News Amsterdam* (www.gay news.nl), in English and Dutch, which have info on gay and lesbian-friendly venues and events. Otherwise, call the **Gay & Lesbian Switchboard** (☎ 623 65 65). If you get into trouble and experience any harassment, contact the **Amsterdam Police Gay Network** (☎ 559 53 85; email:homo network@amsterdam.poli tie.nl).

For Gay Men

ARC (2, C8)

This sleek and stylish bar-restaurant-club has been enormously popular since it first opened. Gorgeous guys line up outside to get in for the great cocktails and even better music. It's jam-packed on weekends.

☎ 689 70 70 ✉ Reguliersdwarsstraat 44 € free

I'LL HAVE WHAT SHE'S HAVING...

A 'coffeeshop' in Amsterdam is in the business of serving cannabis, not cappuccinos (although you can get those too). Coffeeshops were legalised in the Netherlands in 1976 as a way of separating marijuana smokers from the users of hard drugs (heroin, cocaine, amphetamines) in a effort to deal with that problem. And it worked. The Netherlands has fewer 'problem' drug users than most other European countries.

Amsterdam's 250 coffeeshops attract locals and tourists alike. All coffeeshops display a smokers' menu detailing the price per gram (or rolled joint) and country of origin. Space cakes and cookies are also sold, but aren't always on the menu because many tourists can't handle them. If you're trying anything for the first time (a joint or a space cake), always ask the staff how much you should try and how long it will take for the effect to kick in. It's advisable not to mix drink and dope, especially with drugs you've not tried before – the results can be unpredictable and you could feel very ill the next day – not a nice way to spend your time in Amsterdam.

🕑 4pm-1am Mon-Thu & Sun, 9pm-3am Fri & Sat ♿ fair

Argos (2, D4)

Amsterdam's oldest leather bar, with its busy basement darkrooms, porn movies and sex parties, is hidden behind blacked-out windows and is for serious players only.
☎ 662 65 95 ✉ Warmoesstraat 95 € free 🕑 10pm-3am Sun-Thu, 10pm-4am Fri & Sat ♿ fair

Cockring (2, D4)

Leather boys of all ages head to this infamous nightclub well-known for its darkrooms, steamy dance floors, sizzling strip shows and sex parties.
☎ 623 96 04 🖳 www .clubcockring.com ✉ Warmoesstraat 96 € free-€5 🕑 11pm-4am Sun-Thu, 11pm-5am Fri & Sat ♿ fair

De Trut (4, D1)

Gay and lesbian locals (only) head to this alternative club in a grungy basement for cheap Sunday fun. Expect hard dance music, arty events and multimedia performances.
✉ Bilderdijkstraat 165 € €3 🕑 11pm-4am Sun

Entre Nous (2, C8)

The Montmartre (right) crowd generally cruises across to this stylish bar when done belting out ABBA tunes. It gets unbelievably packed late on Friday and Saturday nights.
☎ 623 17 00 ✉ Halvemaansteeg 14 🕑 8pm-3am Sun-Thu, 8pm-4am Fri & Sat ♿ good

Exit (4, D1)

Popular with beautiful gay boys who love Exit's selection of three very different dance floors over three levels, it has *Garbo* nights and a darkroom downstairs that sees lots of action.
☎ 625 87 88 ✉ Reguliersdwarsstraat 42 € free-€5 🕑 11pm-4am Sun-Thu, 11pm-5am Fri & Sat ♿ excellent

Getto (2, D4)

This relaxed bar-restaurant on Warmoesstraat does great cocktails and cheap food, making it the perfect place to start a long night. The two-for-one daily happy hour, from 5pm to 7pm, is an institution.
☎ 421 51 51 🖳 www .getto.nl ✉ Warmoesstraat 51 € free 🕑 Tue-Sun 5pm-1am ♿ poor

Montmartre (2, D8)

One visit will tell you why Montmartre is consistently voted the Netherlands' most popular gay bar – it may be tiny but it doesn't get more camp or more outrageously fun than this. Practise your Kylie and ABBA lyrics before coming.
☎ 620 76 22 ✉ Halvemaansteeg 17 € free 🕑 5pm-1am Mon-Thu & Sun, 5pm-3am Fri & Sat ♿ excellent

Get into Getto for a beer or two

Prik (2, B4)

Amsterdam's newest gay bar was just hitting its stride at the time of writing. It's chic, with lots of crimson leather seating, glam blue walls and funky lighting. Managing to pull off being hip and homely, its party nights are a blast. It's a great 'drop by for a casual drink' kind of bar.
🖳 www.prikamsterdam.nl ✉ Spuistraat 109 🕑 4pm-1am Tue-Thu & Sun, 4pm-3am Fri & Sat

Spijkerbar (4, C1)

This sexy cruise bar is popular with locals and tourists alike for its pool, porn and pinball. Their crazily cheap happy hour, daily from 5 to 7pm, pulls the boys in for €1.60 drinks. Their monthly XXX leather nights (Sundays from 7pm) have a wild reputation, but their Saturday bingo nights are equally as popular.

QUEER QUARTERS

Reguliersdwarsstraat (2, B8) Amsterdam's most famous gay street fills with gorgeous guys most summer evenings.

Amstel & Rembrandtplein (2, D8) Lively camp bars line this otherwise touristy square.

Warmoesstraat (2, D4) Hard-core gay bars – leather, rubber, darkrooms and sex competitions – in the red-light district.

☎ 620 59 19 💻 www .spijkerbar.nl ✉ Kerkstraat 4, 🕑 3pm-1am Sun-Thu, 1pm-3am Fri & Sat

Soho (4, D1)
Perpetually crowded, this kitsch split-level place attracts gorgeous young guys as well as a more mature, sophisticated bunch of gents. ☎ 330 44 00 ✉ Reguliersdwarsstraat 36 € free 🕑 8pm-3am Mon-Thu, to 4am Fri & Sat, 5pm-3am Sun 🚻 excellent

The Other Side (2, B8)
Gay and straight men and women love this gay-run coffeeshop for its bright, clean interior, happy music, great weed and outdoor seats that are well placed for people-watching. Plays a mix of disco, funk and soul, and sells hash, weed and energy drinks. ☎ 421 10 14 ✉ Reguliersdwarsstraat 6 € free 🕑 11am-1am 🚻 good

For Women

Saarein II (3, B5)
Saarein II was a focal point for the feminist movement in the 1970s and has remained popular ever since. Set in a grand old building, it welcomes gay and straight women and men of all ages, although it's primarily a lesbian meeting place. ☎ 623 49 01 ✉ Elandsstraat 119 € free 🕑 5pm-1am Tue-Thu & Sun, to 2am Fri & Sat 🚻 fair

Sappho (4, D1)
Friday is the big night at Sappho, when this usually relaxed place teems with lesbians looking to have a good time. They also have live music and film nights. ☎ 423 15 09 💻 www .sappho.nl ✉ Vijzelstraat 103 € free 🕑 Sun-Thu 3pm-1am, to 3am Fri & Sat 🚻 good

Sugar (3, B5)
Any bar that sells Duvel beer is fine by us! This friendly open-minded girl bar, close to Saarein II (left), is fairly laid-back in the afternoon but can get pretty hot and sultry late at night. ✉ Hazenstraat 19 € €3 🕑 4pm-1am Mon & Wed-Fri, 4pm-3am Sat & Sun 🚻 good

Vivelavie (2, D8)
Amsterdam's most popular lesbian bar has friendly bar staff, great music, and a lovely summer terrace. It's a great place for a late drink. ☎ 624 01 14 ✉ Amstelstraat 7 € free 🕑 3pm-1am Sun-Thu, 3pm-3am Fri & Sat 🚻 excellent

Inside the Other Side

SPORT

Football (soccer) is the Netherlands' sport of choice, but there are other sports for the keen observer to get fired up about.

Football

The enormous **ArenA Stadium** (1, C5; ☎ 311 13 33; Arena Boulevard 29, Bijlmer) is home ground to the Netherlands' top team, Ajax. They play from September to June, with a winter break from Christmas to February. The high-tech complex seats 52,000 spectators and has a snazzy retractable roof and interactive museum complete with football paraphernalia, films and multimedia presentations. Games generally take place Saturday evening and Sunday afternoon.

ALL STEAMED UP

Thermos Day Sauna and Thermos Night Sauna have been keeping things steamy for decades. The sprawling **day sauna** (☎ 623 91 58; www.thermos .nl; Raamstraat 33; admission €18; ☾ noon-11pm Mon-Fri, to 10pm Sat, 11am-10pm Sun) offers a Turkish bath, Finnish dry sauna, hair and beauty salon, restaurant and bar, roof terrace, and 'relax cabins'. The nearby **night sauna** (☎ 623 49 36; Kerkstraat 58-60; admission €18; ☾ 11pm-8am Sun-Fri, to 10am Sat) is equipped with baths and saunas and lots of sweaty 'relaxation rooms' for keeping the heat up high.

Hockey

The Dutch (field) hockey team is among the world's best and the season runs between September and May. Contact **Hockey Club Hurley** (☎ 619 02 33; Nieuwe Kalfjeslaan 21, Amsterdamse Bos) for information and to find out when international events are being held at the 7000-seat Wagener Stadium. Match details are also available online at www.knhb.nl.

Korfball

Korfball is an unusual cross between netball, volleyball and basketball. First-time spectators are easily identified at games – they're the ones snickering. Mixed-sex teams attempt to throw a ball into the opposing team's hoop. Players can only mark opponents of the same sex. There's an enormously popular local club scene and a long season that incorporates both field and indoor games. Contact the **Amsterdam Sport Council** (☎ 552 24 90) for further information or check online at www.noordwest.knkv.nl.

Clean up at the ArenA Stadium, home ground to Ajax

Sleeping

This being Amsterdam, the accommodation scene is as eclectic as you'd expect. There is everything from the whisper-quietly-in-your-ear discretion of Seven One Seven (p101), to the bondage bounty of the Black Tulip Hotel (p101). However, having enough room to swing a cat-o'-nine-tails is an issue in Amsterdam, as space is an expensive commodity, especially on the canals. Hotels tend to be small – anything with over 20 rooms is *big* – and the rooms themselves are often snug. During spring and summer, the less expensive accommodation books out fast, so reserve well ahead.

> **ROOM RATES**
> The categories in this guide indicate the cost per night of a standard double room.
>
> | | |
> |---|---|
> | Deluxe | over €240 |
> | Top End | €140-240 |
> | Midrange | €90-139 |
> | Budget | under €90 |

In a city that is best traversed on foot or bike, location is king. It is definitely worth paying a little extra to be in the heart of things – or not much further out than the Museumplein area or around the Vondelpark, as you'll find that while it's more tranquil, you'll miss the energy of the city centre.

Top-end and deluxe hotels all have rooms with private bathrooms, whereas this was not always true in less expensive options. Many hotels have narrow, steep stairs with no elevators (lifts), which can make them inconvenient. While all hotels have heating, many places do not have air-conditioning due to the short summer but it can still get uncomfortable in July and August – and those canal mosquitoes can really leave their mark when you leave the window open.

The efficient www.bookings.nl is your best online hotel-booking option; bookings are free and you receive confirmation in seconds. If you're not so well prepared, same-day hotel bookings can be made at **VVV** (2, E2; ☎ 201 88 00; Centraal Station; ☯ 8am-8pm Mon-Thu & Sat, 8am-9pm Fri, 9am-5pm Sun) and **GWK** (2, E2; ☎ 627 27 31; Centraal Station; ☯ 8am-10pm Mon-Sat, 9am-10pm Sun). Note that many hotels charge up to 5% extra if you wish to pay by credit card.

DELUXE

Banks Mansion Amsterdam (2, C9)

After opening in 2004, this former bank has become one of Amsterdam's most highly regarded hotels. The 51 rooms here vary in size, but all are contemporary, with Art Deco touches appealingly blending with mod cons such as plasma-screen TVs. Breakfast, drinks and snacks are inclusive.

☎ 420 00 55 ▯ www .banksmansion.nl ✉ Herengracht 519-525 ⚒ ▯ ♿

Dylan Amsterdam (5, C4)

The hotel, formerly known as Blakes, is an effortlessly chic affair on the lovely Keizersgracht – perfect for shopping. A conversion of 17th-century canal houses, its 41 rooms feature decor in several styles and colours, such as the raspberry red of the 'Klassbols' to the black lacquer of the 'Kimono'.

☎ 530 20 10 ▯ www .dylanamsterdam.com

IN A WORD...

- Business – InterContinental Amstel Amsterdam (opposite)
- Romantic – Hotel Pulitzer (right)
- Location – Hotel de l'Europe (below)
- Stylish – Banks Mansion Amsterdam (left)
- Outrageous – Black Tulip Hotel (opposite)

✉ Keizersgracht 384 ♿ excellent ⚒ ▯ ✂ ♿

Grand Amsterdam Sofitel Demeure (2, C6)

A hotel fit for a queen (Queen Beatrix was married here), this is one of Amsterdam's most regal addresses. This former town hall (1808–1987) is home to some grandiose public spaces and vast guest rooms with excellent canal views. Café Roux serves up unapologetically old-fashioned French cuisine.

☎ 555 31 11 ▯ www .thegrand.nl ✉ Oudezijds Voorburgwal 197 ♿ excellent ⚒ ▯ ✂ ♿

Hotel de l'Europe (2, C7)

This elegant Victorian hotel dating from 1899 has an unsurpassable location offering commanding views of the Amstel River. While all the rooms here are handsome, take advantage of the location and pay the extra for an Amstel view room. In summer the terrace café, La Terrasse, is a must-do.

☎ 531 17 77 ▯ www .leurope.nl ✉ Nieuwe Doelenstraat 2-8 ♿ fair ⚒ ▯ ✂ ▦ ♿

Hotel Pulitzer (3, B4)

Comprising 230 beautiful rooms spread over 25 17th-century canal houses, the Pulitzer pulls off the admirable feat of still feeling boutique. The canal- or garden-view rooms come with all the mod cons, with everything from a cigar bar to a 24-hour fitness centre – and the prettiest

Stand tall at the Hotel de L'Europe

boat touring Amsterdam's canals!
☎ 523 52 35 🖳 www .pulitzer.nl ✉ Prinsengracht 315-331 🔀 🖳 ✂ ♿

InterContinental Amstel Amsterdam (4, F3)
Old-school elegance abounds at this extravagant marble-and-crystal festooned hotel, which opened its doors in 1867. Impeccable service, fantastic facilities (including a superlative gym and spa), it's a safe bet for the fussiest traveller. Its **La Rive** (p74) restaurant serves up some of the best French/Mediterranean food in town.
☎ 622 60 60 🖳 www .interconti.com ✉ Professor Tulpplein 1 ♿ excellent 🖳 ✂ ♿

Seven One Seven (4, C1)
Seven One Seven does one-on-one service like no other. This classical 19th-century guesthouse has only eight rooms; two massive executive suites, four huge junior suites and two generous deluxe rooms, all sumptuously decorated and featuring intriguing *objets d'art*. Pitch-perfect for those craving the home-away-from-home treatment.
☎ 427 07 17 🖳 www .717hotel.nl ✉ Prinsengracht 717 🔀 🖳

TOP END

Ambassade Hotel (2, A7)
A tasteful treat across 10 17th-century canalside houses, the 59 individually decorated rooms here ooze style. Many rooms feature Herengracht or Singel canal views and all have great

Bed down at Bilderberg Hotel Jan Luyken

amenities including broadband internet access. Signed authors' works in its library are testament to its reputation as *the* literary address in Amsterdam.
☎ 555 02 22 🖳 www .ambassade-hotel.nl ✉ Herengracht 341 ♿ fair 🔀 🖳 ✂ ♿

Bilderberg Hotel Jan Luyken (4, B3)
For museum lovers on a mission, this understated boutique hotel located between the Rijksmuseum and the Vondelpark is perfectly positioned. While there are 62 rooms (some are a little tight), it's a discreet and quiet address and has the feel of a much smaller hotel.
☎ 573 07 30 🖳 www .janluyken.nl ✉ Jan Luijkenstraat 58 ♿ fair ♿

Black Tulip Hotel (2, E3)
This canalside, centrally located hotel has nine excellent rooms with cable TV and wi-fi; seven with extra odd cons including sling-and-bondage hooks, fisting chairs and whipping benches. Well, what did you expect from an exclusively gay-male hotel

kitted out for bondage? Don't forget your safe word.
☎ 427 09 33 🖳 www .blacktulip.nl ✉ Gelderskade 16 ♿ good 🖳

College Hotel (4, B5)
This former late-19th-century school is one cool Amsterdam address – despite being too far from the action for some. With its low-key tones and understated style, along with flatscreen TVs and wi-fi, what sets it apart is the hospitality students that staff it – which is preferable to out-of-work models...
☎ 571 15 11 🖳 www .thecollegehotel.com ✉ Roelof Hartstraat 1 ♿ excellent 🔀 🖳 ✂ ♿

Hotel Toren (2, A3)
This excellent address on lovely Keizersgracht is perfect for those seeking the charm of a Golden Age era property. It's close to the action but very peaceful at night, and the staff are friendly. Go for a deluxe room in their main building for a fantastic view over the canal.
☎ 622 63 52 🖳 www .hoteltoren.nl ✉ Keizersgracht 164 🔀 🖳

Hotel Vondel (4, B2)
This stylish, understated hotel is in a quiet location five minutes' walk from both the Rijksmuseum and the Leidseplein. Rooms range from small doubles to a suite, the best being the Vondel rooms which are large doubles. There are all mod cons (including wi-fi), nonsmoking rooms, and a chic bar.
☎ 612 01 20 ☐ www .hotelvondel.nl ✉ Vondel-straat 28-30 ☐ ✗ ♿

Lloyd Hotel (1, E3)
Without doubt, Amsterdam's most contentious hotel. Whether you'll enjoy this former migrant hotel depends on your reaction to this; you need to catch a tram to it, its 116 rooms span from one- to five-star, it has a 'Cultural Embassy' and some rooms have a shower in the middle. Both fascinating and infuriating.
☎ 561 36 36 ☐ www .lloydhotel.com ✉ Oostel-ijke Handelskade 34 ♿ excellent ☐ ♿

NH Hotel Doelen (2, C8)
The Spanish-owned NH chain now appears to own every second hotel in Amsterdam, however, this one is a winner with its excellent location and Old World style. Art history buffs will be keen to know that it has a portion of the wall where Rembrandt painted *The Night Watch*.
☎ 554 06 00 ☐ www .nh-hotels.com ✉ Nieuwe Doelenstraat 24 ♿ fair ☐ ✗ ♿

't hotel (2, A4)
While 't hotel is yet another 17th-century canal house converted to a hotel, this one's a winner, with eight comfortable rooms (with canal views) and contemporary furniture that manages to blend well with existing architecture. There is a great buffet breakfast, free wi-fi and a refreshing nonsmoking policy.
☎ 422 27 41 ☐ www .thotel.nl ✉ Leliegracht 18 ☐ ✗ ♿

MIDRANGE

Hotel Amistad (2, C1)
With its flirty slogan 'sleep with us', this renovated gay-focussed hotel gives boys every good reason to do so. Hip (and red) flourishes abound, while the very accommodating breakfast bench is open until 1pm, when it transforms into an internet café. They also rent great apartments and penthouses.
☎ 624 80 74 ☐ www .amistad.nl ✉ Kerkstraat 42 ☐ ✗

Hotel Arena (1, E4)
This former monastery and hostel was converted into a stylish hotel in 2000, and while it appears the gloss has worn off a bit, the groups taking advantage of the bar, club and restaurant don't seem to mind. The location means you'll be catching trams though.
☎ 850 24 00 ☐ www.hotelarena.nl ✉ 's-Gravesandestraat 51 ♿ excellent ☐

Stairway to heaven at the Hotel Arena

Singel & doubles at Hotel Brouwer

Hotel Brouwer (2, B3)
Located in a charming 17th-century canal house on the Singel, this family hotel (since 1917) has been extensively renovated in a refreshingly simple manner with exposed beams and lovely canal views. The six doubles and two singles have been named after Dutch painters from the 17th through 20th centuries.
☎ 624 63 58 ▢ www.hotel brouwer.nl ✉ Singel 83 ✕

Hotel de Filosoof (1, C4)
This thinking person's hotel welcomes brainiacs to its 38 small, but well thought out rooms, each dedicated to a philosopher, writer or thinker. Less cheesy than it sounds and infinitely more interesting, if the lovely garden doesn't allow you to be immersed in thought, head to the nearby Vondelpark.
☎ 683 30 13 ▢ www.hotel filosoof.nl ✉ Anna van den Vondelstraat 6 ♿ fair ♨

Hotel Fita (4, B3)
This 16-room, family-owned hotel is full of happy surprises. A nonsmoking hotel, freshness extends from the well-kept, modern rooms to the great breakfast. The location is perfect for the museums and shopping and with free wi-fi, laundry, telephone calls within Europe and to the USA you're on a winner.
☎ 679 09 76 ▢ www.fita .nl ✉ Jan Luijkenstraat 37 ▢ ✕

Hotel New Amsterdam (2, B2)
Wonderful attention to detail abounds in this renovated 25-room boutique hotel. The little touches in the rooms will bring a smile to your face as will the great canal location, friendly staff and cool clientele. Take a double room with canal view or a suite for best effect.
☎ 522 23 45 ▢ www.hotel newamsterdam.nl ✉ Herengracht 13-19 ♿ fair

Hotel Orlando (4, F2)
This lovely 17th-century canalside boutique hotel has only five rooms. And they are big for central Amsterdam, with high ceilings and décor in an eclectic mix of old and new. There are generous mod cons you'd expect in a five-star (it's a three), such as broadband internet and a minibar.
☎ 638 69 15 ▢ www .hotelorlando.nl ✉ Prinsengracht 1099 ✕ ▢ ✕

Hotel V (1, D5)
This small hotel is a modish number, with a fresh, minimalist style with brilliant flashes of colour and a groovy fireplace. With only 24 understated rooms, it's a personal and personable hotel with enough mod cons (including wi-fi) to keep hipsters happy. Also close to the bars of de Pijp.
☎ 662 32 33 ▢ www .hotelv.nl ✉ Victorieplein 42 ▢

Misc (2, D5)
This quirky little hideaway near the red-light district features six differently decorated rooms; Design, Wonders, Rembrandt, Retro, Afrika and Baroque. Set in a 17th-century canal house, the larger rooms with canal views are the best bet and the breakfast served until noon is a nice touch for night owls.
☎ 330 62 41 ▢ www .hotelmisc.com ✉ Kloveniersburgwal 20 ▢

ROOMS WITH A VIEW
A room overlooking Amsterdam's canals can be both romantic and entertaining. Whether you end up with elegant 16th-century buildings reflected on calm water, or Amsterdammers motoring by sharing some cheese and a bottle of rosé, it's always compelling. Here's where you get some:
- Hotel de l'Europe (p100)
- Ambassade Hotel (p101)
- Hotel Toren (p101)
- Hotel Brouwer (left)

Three colours, Seven Bridges

Piet Hein Hotel (4, A3)
Located close to the museums and overlooking the Vondelpark, this immaculate hotel offers a good variety of rooms (including good single 'business' rooms) in a quiet location. There is a relaxing bar that's open late, wi-fi throughout the hotel and a decent breakfast.
☎ 662 72 05 🖳 www .hotelpiethein.nl ✉ Vossiusstraat 52-53 🖳

Seven Bridges (4, E2)
Named after the seven bridges within sight of this lovely hotel, this place has a wonderful, slightly eccentric ambience as well as divine vistas. The eight discerningly decorated rooms feature oriental rugs and elegant antiques – don't bother looking for the breakfast room, it's breakfast in bed here!
☎ 623 13 29 🖳 www.seven bridgeshotel.nl ✉ Reguliersgracht 31 🖳 ♿

BUDGET

Hotel Bema (4, B4)
While this informal hotel feels somewhat out of place in the

upmarket neighbourhood by the Concertgebouw, its funky feel is most certainly welcome. In addition to the clean, simple rooms it also has apartments available.
☎ 679 13 96 🖳 www .bemahotel.com ✉ Concertgebouwplein 19b 🖳 ♿

Hotel Kap (4, D3)
On a quiet residential street is this simple, clean, well-run hotel with 15 rooms, most with their own bathroom. There's an attractive courtyard garden and breakfast room, and the museum district, markets and bars are a short walk away.
☎ 624 59 08 🖳 www .kaphotel.nl ✉ Den Texstraat 5b 🖳

Hotel Prinsenhof (4, E2)
Located off lively Utrechtse straat, the generously sized spotless rooms (the attic rooms are charming) and friendly welcome are a breath of fresh air in this category. At present only a couple of rooms have full private facilities, so book ahead.
☎ 623 17 72 🖳 www .hotelprinsenhof.com

✉ Prinsengracht 810 ♿ fair ♿

Hotel Rembrandt (5, A5)
One of the best value hotels in Amsterdam, the Rembrandt is located in a leafy residential area near the Artis Zoo (p22). Rooms are spick and span, with TV, phone and coffee/tea making facilities, but the best feature is the stunning breakfast room, with its 17th-century paintings.
☎ 627 27 14 🖳 www .hotelrembrandt.nl ✉ Plantage Middenlaan 17 ♿ good ♿

International Budget Hostel (4, B1)
What we like most about this popular hostel is the fabulous canalside location, just a short stroll to some great bars and coffeeshops. The hostel lounge is great for chilling with the other guests. The only downside here is, being a 17th-century building, the rooms are a little tight.
☎ 624 27 84 🖳 www.inter nationalbudgethostel.com ✉ Leidsegracht 76 🖳 ✉

About Amsterdam

HISTORY

While the oldest archaeological finds in Amsterdam date from Roman times, there's no evidence that there was a settlement in these waterlogged swamplands. It took the pioneering peasants living on the banks of the River IJ (pronounced 'eye') to settle, building the first dams in 1150. Soon there emerged a fishing village known as Aemstelredamme ('dam built across the River Amstel') at what is now Dam Square, and in 1275 the village of Amsterdam was officially born.

Independent Republic

During the Reformation in the 15th century, the stern Calvinist movement took hold in the 17 provinces of the Low Countries. This was integral to the region's struggle against the fanatical rule (and the Spanish Inquisition) of the Catholic Philip II of Spain. In 1578 Calvinist brigands captured Amsterdam in a bloodless coup and the northern provinces declared themselves an independent republic.

The Golden Age

When trading rival Antwerp (now in Belgium) was retaken by the Spaniards in the late 16th century, merchants, skippers and artisans flocked to Amsterdam, and a new moneyed society emerged, trade-based but intellectual. The world's first regular newspaper was printed here in 1618. Persecuted Jews from Portugal and Spain also fled to Amsterdam; they knew of trade routes to the West and East Indies, introduced the diamond industry (fed by Brazilian gems) and made Amsterdam a tobacco centre. The city grew apace: the population quadrupled to 220,000 in the 100 years to 1700. The Dutch dominated in sea trade over other European powers, giving them a virtual monopoly on North Sea fishing and Arctic whaling.

Nieuwe Kerk (p26-7): well, it was new in the 15th century

Declining Fortunes

By the late 17th century, Holland didn't have the resources to match the growing might of France and England. Dutch merchants began to invest their fortunes in secure ventures, rather than daring sea voyages and innovation. The result was stagnation, with wealth generated via interest rates. The mighty United East India Company, which once controlled European trade with Asia, went bankrupt in 1800.

New Infrastructure

Amsterdam shook off its torpor when Holland's first railway opened in 1839. Major infrastructure projects formed the backbone of Amsterdam's economy. Canal links to the North Sea and the Rhine River helped the city benefit from the Industrial Revolution. The harbour was expanded, the diamond industry boomed and Amsterdam's population passed the half-million mark by 1900.

WWII & the Postwar Period

During WWII, Amsterdam experienced war for the first time in almost four centuries. The Jewish population of Amsterdam, estimated at 80,000, were sent to concentration camps and while some Jews managed to hide, such as Anne Frank (p10), by the end of the war there were only 5000 Jews left in Amsterdam. The harsh winter of 1944–45 brought severe famine and thousands died. After WWII, with US aid and the discovery of new natural-gas fields, the city's growth resumed.

Amsterdam Today

The economic growth of the 1950s led to a cultural revolution in the '60s (and more than a little flower power) that swept away the days of autocratic government. Grandiose housing schemes were hatched and many old neighbourhoods were demolished. By the '90s the city had changed radically: the centre was now dominated by a booming service industry and white-collar professionals. Amsterdam won back the economic status that had eluded it since the Golden Age. Yet, despite creeping gentrification, Amsterdam retains its easy cosmopolitan feel thanks to its multicultural mix, with nearly half the city's residents hailing from abroad, the largest groups from Surinam, Morocco and Turkey.

ENVIRONMENT

Green issues are paramount in Western Europe's most densely populated country, which has 16 million people in a far smaller space than the Republic of Ireland (which has approximately four million people). The canals are cleaner today than they've ever been, and use of environmentally friendly natural gas has cleared the air. Industrial pollution is kept firmly in check with some of the strictest regulations in the world. Amsterdam's famous canals are flushed daily to help keep them clean and 60-odd fish species – saltwater, freshwater and brackish types – still manage to survive.

The inner city has become a much more pleasant place for pedestrians since the mid-1980s thanks to the council's efforts to curb the number of cars in town. The number of parking spaces is strongly curtailed and cars are actively discouraged.

GOVERNMENT & POLITICS

Amsterdam is the Dutch capital, however parliament and the seat of government are in The Hague. Queen Beatrix is formally the head of state, but her function is largely symbolic as the Netherlands has been a parliamentary democracy since the mid-19th century. Federally, the Christian Democratic Party (centre-right) has been in power since 2002, but elections were due in November 2006 following the collapse of the government after an internal dispute over contentious Immigration Minister Rita Verdonk.

Amsterdam itself has been a left-wing city ever since its residents won the vote. After the 2006 local elections, the Labour Party (PvdA) and the

DID YOU KNOW?

- Amsterdam's population is 744,736 with 174 nationalities represented
- Amsterdammers own 600,000 bicycles
- There are more than 400km of bicycle paths in the city
- There are 211 coffeeshops and 86 'hash bars' (selling both soft drugs and alcohol)
- Coffeeshops are licensed to sell 5g of marijuana to those over 18
- Only 5% of Amsterdam's coffeeshop customers are Dutch
- Only 10% of Dutch people own their own homes
- The Netherlands is the world's third most densely populated country after Bangladesh and South Korea
- 25% of the country would be under water if the dams burst
- The British visit Amsterdam in the greatest numbers, followed by Americans, Germans, Italians and the Spanish

green Groen Links party linked up for the first time to govern under a 'People make Amsterdam' slogan. This city council and municipal executive oversee the city's 15 boroughs, each with its own district council and executive committee. The 45 council members are elected every four years (the next election will be in 2010), while oddly, the mayor is appointed by the Crown for a period of six years. The districts have a great deal of autonomy, hence services can vary markedly between neighbourhoods.

ECONOMY

Amsterdam has been the Netherlands' economic powerhouse since the Industrial Revolution. In the 1960s and '70s, worsening congestion and environmental issues forced many industries to seek areas with fewer constraints. However, the canal city bounced back, reinventing its role as a trade and financial services centre.

From 1980 until 2000, the Netherlands was Europe's economic miracle. All that changed in 2002, with the country entering its first recession in 20 years. Unemployment ballooned from 2% to 6% (Amsterdam's unemployment rate hovers just under 10%). However by 2006, the Netherlands was experiencing a period of strong growth – especially compared to other European countries. The main economic sectors employ roughly equal numbers of people: manufacturing; commerce and finance; tourism; and science, arts and crafts. Tourism generates a turnover of almost one billion euros per year and employs around 9% of the workforce.

SOCIETY & CULTURE

The Netherlands – and Amsterdam in particular – pushes the envelope on moral and social issues (drugs, abortion, euthanasia and homosexuality), as they believe it's pointless to try to eradicate activities such as drug use and prostitution. The pragmatic approach to drug use in Amsterdam is the one that gets the most attention. Despite the notion that soft drugs inevitably leads to harder ones, it's not borne out in statistics – with the UK having nearly double the number of people who have tried cocaine,

NETHERLANDS/HOLLAND/DUTCH?

While the Dutch don't mind their country being called Holland (especially if they're winning a football match at the time!), Holland is actually a region in the west of the country. The correct name for the country is 'the Netherlands'. The term 'Low Countries' which you might hear, technically refers to Belgium and Luxembourg as well – or Benelux – (Be)lgium, the (Ne)therlands and (Lux)embourg. The three-country Benelux is a free-trade area that served as a model for the EU, of which the Dutch are founding members. The country's people and language are called Dutch.

for instance. In addition, the rates of usage of soft drugs such as cannabis is no higher than most countries in Europe.

Etiquette

Amsterdammers are a pretty relaxed bunch and this is reflected in their casual dress. Slightly smarter casual wear is appropriate at the theatre, opera or more upmarket restaurants; formal dress is reserved for business and bank dealings.

The accepted greeting is a handshake. Cheek-kissing (two or three pecks) is common between people who know one another socially. If you're invited home for dinner, bring something for the host: a bunch of flowers or a plant, a bottle of wine, cake or pastries. It's polite to arrive five to 15 minutes late (never early and *definitely* no later), but business meetings start on time.

The Dutch can be stunningly blunt; it seems it hardly matters how you say something, it's what you say that counts. At the same time, they also have an unusual ability to laugh at themselves and lampoon people who take themselves too seriously.

For such a forward-thinking group, it's surprising that Amsterdammers place few restrictions on cigarette smoking and few will ever ask if you mind if they smoke. Smoking dope in many public places is frowned upon, and you'll find that Amsterdam's liberalism doesn't extend to just lighting up a joint anywhere you want.

ARTS

Almost since its founding, Amsterdam has been a major trendsetting centre of the arts. It lacked a powerful court and wealthy church, but compensated with a large middle class that were great sponsors of the arts. So it comes as little surprise that Amsterdam's international renown lies chiefly in painting and architecture.

Art & Architecture

Most people associate Dutch art with Golden Age painters such as Rembrandt, Vermeer and Frans Hals. Amsterdam also has a wealth of works by Flemish masters such as Pieter Bruegel and Hieronymus Bosch, as the entire region was once part of the Low Countries. Other local legends include Jacob van Ruysdael, Albert Cuyp, Jan Steen, Cornelis Troost and Jacob de Wit. The 19th-century Dutch master Vincent van Gogh is arguably the most famous painter of all time.

In the modern era, the works of visual wizards such as Piet Mondrian (best known artist of the de Stijl movement), HP Berlage and MC Escher help to uphold Amsterdam's reputation for innovative painting, architecture and graphic arts respectively. More recently, Amsterdam has become known for its furniture and product design.

Music

Amsterdam has contributed little to the world's musical and theatrical heritage, but the promotion of cultural events in a city this size is unparalleled. The Concertgebouw (p28) prides itself on a world-class symphony orchestra, and top local and international talents headline in the local music clubs. A handful of pop groups with a wide following hails from here, although it's been decades since names such as Golden Earring, Shocking Blue or the George Baker Selection first shot to fame in the late '60s and early '70s.

The city once had a lively punk music scene but, after a flirtation with guitar-driven rock bands in the '80s, it has evolved into a centre for house, techno and R&B. 'Gabber' or 'Gabba', is a sub-genre of hardcore techno music that started in the early 1990s in Rotterdam. An overdriven bass drum and fast beats (rarely under 160 BPM) are the signatures of this style and it's had a resurgence in popularity lately, taking a more industrial turn. The city also boasts fantastic hip-hop, ska and world-music scenes.

HEY, I KNOW THAT SONG!

Don't know any music from Amsterdam or Holland? Check these out and if you don't recognise them, raid your parent's record collection!

- *Little Green Bag* – The George Baker Selection's 1970 hit had a driving bass line and a catchy chorus. We can almost forgive him for *Una Paloma Blanca*, the hit from 1975. Almost.
- *Radar Love* – Golden Earring's big hit from 1973 was rock 'n' roll personified, the best driving song ever, and clocked in at over six minutes – very radio-unfriendly!
- *Venus* – Shocking Blue's big hit from 1970 was later a hit for girl-group Bananarama in 1986.

Directory

ARRIVAL & DEPARTURE

Air

Amsterdam's Schiphol International Airport (AMS; 6, E3), 18km southwest of the city centre, handles nearly 50 million passengers a year, as Europe's fourth-largest airport. The arrivals area is on the ground floor in the Schiphol Plaza; take a left out of the passenger area to visit the **Holland Tourist Information office** (⏱ 7am-10pm). The departure hall is upstairs — arrive early, as the tax-free shopping here is great value.

INFORMATION

For airport and flight information, call ☎ 0900-0141 (€0.40 per minute) or check www.schiphol.nl. The P1 and P2 short-term carparks charge €1.90 per half-hour for the first three hours and €2.70 for every hour thereafter. The P3 long-term parking area is a fair distance from the terminal but linked by a free 24-hour shuttle bus; parking costs €50 for the first three days (minimum charge) and €5.50 per day thereafter.

AIRPORT ACCESS

Train

From 6am to midnight, trains run to Centraal Station every 15 minutes. The service takes 15 to 20 minutes and costs €3.60.

Bus

Airport shuttle bus company **Connexion** (☎ 38 3394741; www.airporthotelshuttle .nl) will drop you at your hotel door. It costs €12/19 one way/return, and leaves from platform A7 every 15 minutes from 6am to 9pm.

Taxi

A taxi to the city centre takes 20 to 30 minutes (longer in rush hour) and costs about €35 to €45.

Train

Amsterdam's main train station, Centraal Station, has regular and efficient connections to most destinations within the Netherlands and in neighbouring countries. International train information and reservations can be found at the always busy **NS International Reservations Office** (Centraal Station; www.ns.nl; ⏱ 7am-10pm). Alternatively you can buy international tickets online using a credit card and pick them up at the station. For information only, call the less reliable **Teleservice NS Internationaal** (☎ 0900-9296; per min €0.40). Reserve international seats in advance in peak periods, however for travel within Holland, just turn up at the station; you'll rarely have to wait more than an hour for a train. Tickets must be purchased before boarding.

Bus

The most extensive European bus network is **Eurolines** (2, C5; ☎ 560 87 88; www .eurolines.com; Rokin 10), near Dam Square. You can buy tickets at most travel agencies and at the Netherlands Railways Reisburo, Centraal Station. Buses leave from the **Eurolines bus station** (1, E5; ☎ 694 56 31) next to Amstelstation; give yourself 30 minutes to get there from Centraal Station on the metro (five stops).

CLIMATE CHANGE & TRAVEL

Travel – especially air travel – is a significant contributor to global climate change. At Lonely Planet, we believe that all travellers have a responsibility to limit their personal impact. As a result, we have teamed with Rough Guides and other concerned industry partners to support Climatecare.org, which allows travellers to offset the greenhouse gases they are responsible for with contributions to sustainable travel schemes. Lonely Planet offsets all staff and author travel. For more information, check out www.lonely planet.com.

Boat

Services between Holland and the UK (as well as some Scandinavian routes) are run by **Stenaline** (☎ 0900-8123; www .stenaline.com), **P&O North Sea Ferries** (☎ 01482-377 177; www.poferries.com) and **DFDS Seaways** (☎ 0990-333 111; www.dfdsseaways.co.uk). Ask for train–boat–train deals.

Travel Documents
PASSPORT

If you're from outside the EU, you must have a passport valid for three months from the date of entry. EU citizens must have a passport or an identity card.

VISA

Visas are not required by EU citizens or by nationals of Australia, Canada, Israel, Japan, South Korea, New Zealand, Singapore and the USA. Nationals of other countries should check with their local Dutch embassy.

Customs & Duty Free

For visitors from EU countries, ceilings only still apply for perfumes and other luxury products. Residents of non-EU European countries can bring in up to 200 cigarettes or 250g (8oz) of tobacco, 2L of wine plus 1L of spirits, 50ml of perfume and 250ml of eau de toilette, and any other goods up to the value of €175. EU citizens can bring in limitless amounts of goods, so long as they're for personal use.

Departure Tax

Departure tax is prepaid, as it's included in the price of your ticket.

Left Luggage

There is a left-luggage counter in the basement at Schiphol airport (⏱ 6.15am-10.15pm); up to 30kg can be left at the staffed counter (€5 per item per day). Lockers are available from €5 to €9 (depending on size) per day and luggage can be stored for up to a week. Left luggage at Centraal Station costs €5 per item for 24 hours.

GETTING AROUND

Amsterdam is a compact city and a wonderful city to walk in, but there's also an efficient public transport system combining tram, bus and metro. While access in the canal belt streets is limited, you rarely need walk more than 1km from a tram or bus stop to your destination.

Most trams and buses converge at Centraal Station. The GVB (Gemeentevervoerbedrijf or Municipal Transport Company) **information office** (2, E2; ☎ 0900-80 11, www.gvb.nl; per min €0.10; ⏱ 7am-9pm Mon-Fri, to 7pm late Oct-Mar, from 8am Sat & Sun), in front of the station, sells tickets and passes. Pick up a free *Tourist Guide to Public Transport* booklet and transport map.

Tickets & Travel Passes

First rule, don't travel without a validated ticket: the Dutch uniformed and plainclothes inspectors have heard the silly foreigner story a million times. The inevitable result is an on-the-spot fine of €37.40.

Instead, buy the handy *strippenkaart* (strip card) from tobacco shops, post offices, train station counters and ticketing machines, many bookshops and newsagents, and outlets of the GVB. It's valid on all buses, trams and metros (but Schiphol airport is not included). It costs €1.60/2.40/6.70/19.80 for 2/3/15/45 strips (children under four travel free, and those up to 11 pay reduced fares) and the minimum you'll use for each journey is two strips. The three-strip ticket is for a single covering two zones.

Amsterdam is divided into five zones (all of the main attractions are in zone one, called Centrum). When you get on a tram, bus or train, you stamp one strip for your journey and one strip for each zone you travel in. If you're travelling in zone one only, you stamp one strip for your journey and one for the zone. If travelling in two zones, you stamp one for your journey and two for the two zones, and so on.

Stamped tickets are valid for one hour. Any number of people can travel on one *strippenkaart*, but the correct number of strips must be stamped. So if two of you are making a short journey within Centrum, you must stamp four strips.

If you're going to use a lot of public transport in one day, get a *dagkaart* (day card), which gives adults/children unlimited travel for €6.30/4.20. Two days is €10 and three €13. (See also p116 for information on combined transport and museum passes.)

Tram

Amsterdam trams are wonderful: fast, efficient and frequent. In the past two years, conductors have been reintroduced on many routes to stop fare evasion and to increase passenger security, so you may have to enter through the rear door, where a conductor will stamp your ticket or sell you one. Exit via any door. There are also *sneltram* (light rail) lines, such as the express one out to IJburg (p30). Most tram lines stop running around midnight.

Bicycle

If you're staying for longer than a couple of days in Amsterdam, hire a bicycle. Riding along a canal on a sunny day is hard to beat, as is the smugness of most of Amsterdam's cyclists, so you're really better off joining them! **Holland Rent-A-Bike** (2, C4; ☎ 622 32 07; Damrak 247), below Beurs van Berlage, has impeccably tuned, non-touristy-looking bikes with reliable locks for €6.50/34.50 per day/week (with €150 or credit card imprint as deposit), as does **Bike City** (5, C2; ☎ 626 37 21; Bloemgracht 68-70), for €8.50/41 with credit card imprint as deposit. Prices are for coaster-brake (not handbrake) bikes. There is a strictly enforced €25 fine for riding through busy Leidsestraat (5, C6) at any time of day or night.

Bus

Buses are the best option for getting to/from the outer suburbs. Board through the front door and show your ticket to the driver. Half-hourly night buses start shortly after midnight and run until 5am Monday to Friday (to 6.30am on weekends).

Metro

Chances are you won't use the metro unless you go to the international bus station at Amstelstation (1, E5) or south to the RAI Convention Centre (1, D5) or the World Trade Centre (1, C5). The metro stops running around midnight.

Ferry

There's a free ferry, marked 'Buiksloterwegveer', running over the IJ to north Amsterdam. It departs from between piers 8 and 9 (2, E1) behind the Centraal Station and runs every five minutes from 6.30am to 9pm, or every 10 minutes from 9pm to 6.30am. The trip takes seven minutes and carries pedestrians and bicycles, though there's not much to do when you arrive.

Canal Boat

The **Lovers Museum Boat** (☎ 622 21 81; www.lovers.nl) leaves every 30 minutes (10am to 6.30pm) from the terminal on **Prins Hendrikkade** (2, D2; opposite No 26, near Centraal Station) stopping at all major museums. A day ticket for unlimited travel costs €15/13, and provides 10% to 50% off at most museums along the route and there is discounts after 1pm. A one-hour canal cruise costs €8.50.

The **Canal Bus** (☎ 623 98 86; www.canal.nl) does a circuit of the tourist centres between Centraal Station and the Rijksmuseum from 10.15am to 6.45pm. A day pass costs €15. Canal 'bikes' (paddleboats, ☎ 626 55 74) can be hired from kiosks at Leidseplein, Keizersgracht/Leidsestraat, the Anne Frank Huis and the Rijksmuseum; two- and four-seaters cost €7 per hour.

Taxi

Flag fall is €3.20, plus €1.90 per kilometre. A 5% to 10% tip is also expected if the driver doesn't get lost. To call a taxi, dial

☎ 677 77 77; there's no extra cost for a phone booking. In theory you must board taxis at taxi stands dotted round the city (Centraal Station, Rembrandtplein and Leidseplein are the biggest), but many will stop if hailed in the street.

Car & Motorcycle

We don't recommend having a car in Amsterdam. Driving on Amsterdam's narrow canalside streets can be a nightmare: parking is expensive, the one-way system is Byzantine and trucks often block the way. Cars with foreign plates risk being broken into and illegally parked vehicles will be clamped with a hefty fine attached.

At most you'll need a car for excursions outside Amsterdam. The rental market is competitive (from €38 per day). The main companies include the following:

Avis (☎ 644 36 84)
Budget (☎ 612 60 66)
Europcar (☎ 683 21 23)

Speed limits are 50km/h in built-up areas, 80km/h in the country, 100km/h on major through roads and 100km/h to 120km/h on freeways (always clearly indicated). The blood-alcohol limit is 0.05%. Drive on the right.

PRACTICALITIES
Business Hours

Most banks and businesses are closed on public holidays. Many shops open on Good Friday and on Christmas and Boxing days. Venues normally closed on Sunday are also likely to be closed on public holidays.
Banks 9am to 4pm Monday to Friday, some till 9pm Thursday and Saturday mornings.
General office hours 8.30am to 5pm Monday to Friday.
Post offices 9am to 6pm Monday to Friday (to 8pm Thursday), 10am to 3pm Saturday.
Restaurants Restaurants open early (around 5.30pm) and most kitchens close by 10pm.

Shops Noon to 6pm Monday, 9am to 6pm Tuesday to Saturday.
Pharmacies Usually 8.30am to 5.30pm Monday to Friday.
Late-night shopping To 9pm Thursday at all larger stores and most smaller stores.

Climate & When to Go

Amsterdam is at its best from May (when the tulips are out) to August (when the days are longest). Accommodation is cheaper from November to December and can fall to ludicrously low levels in the bigger hotels in January and February. From December to March there is plenty of wind and horizontal rain, but you can occasionally ice skate on some of the canals!

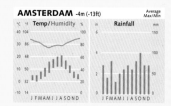

Disabled Travellers

Travellers with reduced mobility will find Amsterdam only moderately well equipped to meet their needs. Most offices, museums and train and metro stations have lifts and/or ramps and toilets for the disabled. However, many budget and midrange hotels are in old buildings with steep stairs and no lifts and hoteliers' hands are tied as entrances to these buildings can't be changed due to their historic value. In addition, the cobbled streets can present problems for wheelchairs. The disabled get discounts on public transport and can park free in designated spots (if they have the appropriate windscreen marker).

INFORMATION & ORGANISATIONS

The **Nederlands Instituut voor Zorg & Welzijn** (NIZW; ☎ 030-230 66 11; www .nizw.nl) has information on accessible places to stay as well as referrals to more specific organisations.

Discounts

STUDENT & YOUTH CARDS

For sightseers under 26, the **Cultureel Jongeren Passport** (CJP, Cultural Youth Pass; www.cjp.nl; €12.50) is the Dutch version of the Euro<26 card and offers huge discounts to major museums and many cultural events.

SENIORS' CARDS

The minimum age for senior discounts is 65 (60 for partners). They apply to public transport, museum admission, theatres, concerts and more. Proof of age may be required – your passport is best.

DISCOUNT CARDS

The **Museumjaarkaart** (Museum Card; over/under 26 €30/15 plus €4.95 administration charge) gives free admission to over 400 museums and galleries across the Netherlands, including many of the ones listed in this book. It's valid for one year and you'll need a passport photo.

If you'll be using public transport, an **I Amsterdam Pass** (1/2/3 days €33/43/53) gets you into all of the big galleries and museums and includes bus, tram and train journeys and a free trip on a canal boat. It also gives discounts to some restaurants. Both cards are available from the VVV and AUB (see p120).

Electricity

If you need an adapter, try to get it at home first because most of those sold in the Netherlands are for locals going abroad.

Cycle AC.
Frequency 50 Hz.
Plugs Standard Continental two round pins.
Voltage 220V.

Embassies & Consulates

Amsterdam may be the country's capital but the government and ministries are based in The Hague, so that's where the embassies are.

Emergencies

In a life-threatening emergency, the national telephone number for ambulance, police and the fire brigade is ☎ 112. For nonemergency police matters, phone ☎ 622 22 22. The Rape Crisis Line is ☎ 613 02 45.

SAFETY CONCERNS

Amsterdam is pretty safe despite the commercial sex and soft drugs. All the same, take special care at night in the red-light district, and in crowded areas such as Centraal Station, Damrak or Leidseplein, where pickpockets operate. The most likely crime you could face is having your bicycle stolen, if you've hired one. Always – *always*, no matter how short a time you're taking your eyes off it – lock up your bicycle with a good lock. And when crossing the street always look for speeding bikes – or the 'silent killers', as we like to call them.

Fitness

GYMS

When the weather's agreeable, it's popular to hit the Vondelpark with your obligatory iPod for a run. At other times locals hit the indoor fitness facilities to work off that beer. A couple to try:

Barry's Health Centre (3, D3; ☎ 626 10 36; www.barryshealthcentre.nl; Lijnbaansgracht 350; day/week pass €15/27.50)

Fitness First (2, C3; ☎ 530 03 40; www.fitnessfirst.nl; Nieuwezijds Kolk 15; day pass €16, monthly pass from €29)

SWIMMING

The city's best facilities for those with little ones is Mirandabad (p35). Nearly as good is the **Marnixbad** (5, B1; ☎ 625 48 43; Marnixplein 5-9; ☺ 10am-4pm Mon-Sat). Ring ahead for evening times. For steamy delights try **Sauna Deco** (2, B3; ☎ 623 82 15; Herengracht 115; admission €15.50, or €12.50 noon-3pm Mon-Fri), a classy Art Deco Scandinavian-style unisex sauna – not a gay venue.

Gay & Lesbian Travellers

Some estimates put Amsterdam's gay and lesbian population between 20% and 30%. Whatever the true figure, the Netherlands has lead the way in gay rights and was the first country in the world to allow same-sex marriages. The age of homosexual consent is 16. Amsterdam's numerous gay and lesbian venues tend to be very visible and welcoming to visitors (see p95).

INFORMATION & ORGANISATIONS

The government-subsidised **COC Amsterdam** (5, C3; ☎ 623 40 79; www.cocamsterdam.nl; Rozenstraat 14) is one of the world's largest gay and lesbian rights organisations. There's also a **Gay & Lesbian Switchboard** (☎ 623 65 65; www.switchboard.nl; ☿ noon-10pm Mon-Fri, 4-8pm Sat & Sun) which is the best place to start for gay and lesbian information in Amsterdam.

Health

No immunisations are needed to visit the Netherlands. Tap water in Amsterdam is safe to drink. Condoms are readily available in pharmacies and supermarkets.

MEDICAL SERVICES

Travel insurance is advisable to cover any medical treatment you may need while in Amsterdam. However, the Netherlands has reciprocal medical schemes with other EU countries and Australia; check with your public health insurer to find out which form to take along. If you have to pay on the spot (and it can be very expensive) you'll be able to claim back home. Citizens from other countries should ensure that they have complete travel/medical insurance coverage.

Call ☎ 0900-503 20 42 (24 hours) for **Centraal Doktordienst**, an English-speaking service that will refer you to an appropriate doctor, dentist or pharmacy. For less urgent medical matters contact **GG&GD** (Municipal Medical & Health Service; 2, D7; ☎ 555 58 22; Groenburgwal 44).

Hospitals with 24-hour emergency units include the following:

Onze Lieve Vrouwe Gasthuis (1, E4; ☎ 599 91 11; Eerste Oosterparkstraat 1; tram 9, 14 or bus 59, 120, 126)
St Lucas Ziekenhuis (1, B3; ☎ 510 89 11; Jan Tooropstraat 164; tram 13, bus 19, 64 or train to Station de Vluchtlaan)
Slotervaart Ziekenhuis (1, A5; ☎ 512 93 33; Louwesweg 6)

PHARMACIES

The local *drogist* (pharmacist) can fill prescriptions or deal with minor health concerns. Dutch speakers can ring ☎ 694 87 09 for a recorded list of 24-hour chemists; otherwise check newspapers or notices in pharmacy windows.

Dam Apotheek (2, C5; ☎ 624 43 31; Damstraat 2; ☿ 8.30am-6pm Mon-Fri, to 5pm Sat) is off Dam Sq.

Holidays

Nieuwjaarsdag (New Year's Day) 1 January
Pasen (Easter) March/April, includes Goede Vrijdag (Good Friday), Eerste and Tweede Paasdag (Easter Sunday and Monday)
Koninginnedag (Queen's Day) 30 April
Hemelvaartsdag (Ascension Day) mid- to late May
Eerste and Tweede Pinksterdag (Whit Sunday and Monday) late May/early June
Eerste and Tweede Kerstdag (Christmas Day and Boxing Day) 25 and 26 December

Internet

Most hotels offer some form of Internet access. Laptop wielders will occasionally find an open wi-fi hotspot, but not as many as you'd expect for such a switched-on capital.

INTERNET CAFÉS

There are plenty of internet cafés dotted around town, including the following:
Damrak 33 (2, D3)
easyEverything (www.easyeverything.com; 2, C8; Reguliersbreestraat 22; per hr €1-3; ☿ 10am-8pm, to 10pm in summer).

Internet City (2, D3; ☎ 620 12 92; Nieuwendijk 76)

USEFUL WEBSITES

Lonely Planet's website (www.lonelyplanet .com) offers a speedy link to many Dutch websites. Others (in English):

Amsterdam City's English language portal (www.iamsterdam.com)

Special Bite restaurant guide (www .specialbite.nl)

Underwater Amsterdam – alternative listings (www.underwateramsterdam.com)

Lost Property

Gevonden Voor werpen (Lost & Found office; ☎ 557 85 44; ⌚ 24hr) At Centraal Station near the luggage lockers; for items left on trains.

GVB info office (2, E2; ☎ 551 49 11; Prins Hendrikkade 108-114; ⌚ 9.30am-4.30pm Mon-Fri) For items found on buses, trams or the metro.

Police lost-property office (1, E4; ☎ 559 30 05; Stephensonstraat 18; ⌚ 9.30am-3.30pm Mon-Fri)

Metric System

The metric system is standard. The Dutch use commas in decimals, and points to indicate thousands.

TEMPERATURE

$°C = (°F - 32) ÷ 1.8$

$°F = (°C \times 1.8) + 32$

DISTANCE

1in = 2.54cm
1cm = 0.39in
1m = 3.3ft = 1.1yd
1ft = 0.3m
1km = 0.62 miles
1 mile = 1.6km

WEIGHT

1kg = 2.2lb
1lb = 0.45kg
1g = 0.04oz
1oz = 28g

VOLUME

1L = 0.26 US gallons
1 US gallon = 3.8L
1L = 0.22 imperial gallons
1 imperial gallon = 4.55L

Money

ATMS

ATMs are found outside most banks, in the airport halls and in the main hall of Centraal Station.

CHANGING MONEY

Avoid the private exchange booths dotted along Rokin and the Damrak: they're convenient and open late hours but commissions and rates are lousy. Banks and post offices offer official exchange rates with €1 to €2 commission, as do the **Grenswissel-kantoren** (GWK, Border Exchange Offices), with 24-hour offices at **Centraal Station** (☎ 627 27 31; ⌚ 8am-10pm Mon-Sat, 9am-10pm Sun) and **Schiphol airport** (☎ 627 27 31; ⌚ 7am-10pm).

CREDIT CARDS

All major cards are recognised, but Amsterdam is still strongly cash-based and many smaller places, restaurants, bars, even supermarkets do not have credit card payment prefer cash or levy a surcharge. Report lost or stolen cards on the following 24-hour numbers:

American Express (☎ 504 80 00, 504 86 66)

Diners Club (☎ 654 55 11)

MasterCard/Eurocard (☎ 030-283 55 55; Utrecht)

Visa (☎ 660 06 11)

CURRENCY

The local currency is the euro. It comes in €500, €200, €100, €50, €20, €10 and €5 notes. There are also €2 and €1 coins, as well as various smaller coinage. One euro is made up of 100 cents.

TRAVELLERS CHEQUES

Banks charge a commission to exchange cheques. **American Express** (2, C4; ☎ 0800-022 01 00; Damrak 66) and **Thomas Cook** (2, C5; ☎ 0800-022 86 30, for lost/stolen cheques 625 09 22; Dam 23-25 or Leidseplein 31A) do not. Shops, restaurants and hotels prefer cash.

Newspapers & Magazines

European editions of English newspapers such as the *Guardian* and the *Independent* are available at most newsstands. The largest Dutch-language newspaper is *De Telegraaf*, a right-wing sensationalist daily. *De Volkskrant* is a one-time Catholic daily with leftist leanings, and *Het Parool* is an Amsterdam afternoon paper with good cultural and political coverage.

Photography & Video

Like most of Europe and Australia, the Netherlands uses the PAL system, which is incompatible with the American and Japanese NTSC system.

Post

The main **post office** (2, A5; Singel 250; ☺ 9am-7pm Mon-Fri, 9am-noon Sat) is busy, but well organised. Stamps are sold at some newsagents, hotels and museums. Use the mailbox slits marked Overige Postcodes (Other Postal Codes) if you don't hand mail in at a counter.

POSTAL RATES

Letters up to 20g posted priority within Europe cost €0.69. Beyond Europe, letters posted priority cost €0.85.

Radio

Dutch radio programming is quite bland. Hence the BBC links:
BBC Radio 4 (198kHz FM)
BBC Radio 5 (693kHz FM) Sports
Q-music (100.7FM; www.q-music.nl)
Radio 538 (102FM; www.radio538.nl)
Sky Radio (101FM; www.skyradio.nl)

Telephone

There are plenty of public phones, but most accept national phonecards only. Some take credit cards but few accept coins. Calls are time-based and cost €0.10 per 20 seconds for national calls.

PHONECARDS

Post offices and newsagencies sell a wide range of local and international phonecards.

MOBILE PHONES

The Netherlands uses the GSM cellular phone system, compatible with phones sold in the UK, Australia and most of Asia, but not those from North America or Japan. Before you leave home, check that your service provider has a roaming agreement with a local counterpart. Sim cards are readily available, but the sheer array of cards and packages (whether for local or international use) will have you headed to the nearest coffeeshop to forget the whole thing.

COUNTRY & CITY CODES

The country code for the Netherlands is ☎ 31; Amsterdam's area code is ☎ 20.

USEFUL PHONE NUMBERS

International directory inquiries (☎ 0900-84 18)
International operator (☎ 0800-04 10)
Local directory inquiries (☎ 0900-80 08)
Reverse-charge (collect, ☎ 0800-01 01)

Television

Dutch TV is a great cure for insomnia – especially if you don't speak Dutch, but some channels run subtitled English-language sitcoms and movies. You'll also find channels from Belgium, France, Germany, Italy and Spain, Euro-channels with sports and music clips, CNN and BBC World.

Time

The Netherlands is on Central European Time (GMT plus one hour). Clocks are put forward one hour for daylight saving at 2am on the last Sunday in March and go back at 3am on the last Sunday in October.

Tipping

Tipping isn't compulsory, but most people add 5% to 10% in taxis. In restaurants, there's a service charge included; people will round up the total to the nearest euro for smaller bills, and to the nearest €5 for a large bill. A tip of 10% is considered generous. In pubs with outdoor or table service, you can just leave small change on the table. Toilet attendants expect €0.25 to €0.50, although €1 is the rule in some clubs.

Toilets

Bars and department stores or other places are handy to pop into to use the toilet – but be prepared to pay at least €0.25 for the pleasure. But at least these toilets are generally spotless.

Tourist Information

Though always busy, the main tourist information source, the VVV (Vereniging voor VreemdelingenVerkeer – literally, Society for Foreigner Traffic), is extremely helpful. It sells maps, discount passes and theatre tickets, books hotel rooms and answers tourist inquiries. The **GWK currency-exchange office** (☎ 627 27 27; ⏰ 7.45am-10pm) inside Centraal Station also books hotel rooms and is less crowded than the VVV offices.

The VVV has four offices: a busy one in front of **Centraal Station** (2, E2; Stationsplein 10; ⏰ hotel bookings 9am-5pm, transport & ticket information 7am-9pm Mon-Fri, 8am-9pm Sat & Sun); **inside Centraal Station** (Platform 2a; ⏰ 8am-7.45pm Mon-Sat, 9am-5pm Sun); and **Leidseplein** (5, C6; Leidseplein 1; ⏰ 9am-5pm Mon-Sat, to 5.15pm Sun). **Holland Tourist Information** (⏰ 7am-10pm), also VVV, is at Schiphol airport. VVV staff also field phone queries in Dutch, English and German on ☎ 0900-400 40 40 (€0.40 per minute), 9am to 5pm Monday to Friday.

For anything related to entertainment, head to the **Amsterdam Uit Buro** (AUB; 5, C6; ☎ 488 77 78 9; ⏰ 10am-6pm, to 9pm Thu), which has free brochures and sells tickets (with a €1.50 mark-up). Its phone service **Uitlijn** (☎ 0900-01 91; aub@aub.nl; per min €0.40) operates from 9am to 9pm. For bookings from abroad, call the **National Reservations Centre** (☎ +31-70-320 25 00).

Women Travellers

Amsterdam is about as safe as it gets among Europe's major cities, and there's little street harassment. However, at night in the red-light district you might get some unwelcome attention if walking by yourself.

LANGUAGE

Almost every Amsterdammer speaks English. Nonetheless, a few words in Dutch show goodwill, which is always appreciated, and you'll begin to understand more of what's going on.

Basics

Hello.	Dag/Hallo.
Goodbye.	Dag.
See you (again).	Tot ziens.
Yes/No.	Ja/Nee.
Please.	Alstublieft/Al sjeblieft. (polite/informal)
Thank you.	Dank u/Bedankt.
You're welcome.	Geen dank.
Excuse me.	Pardon.
I (don't) understand.	Ik begrijp het (niet).
Do you speak English?	Spreekt u Engels?
Please write it down.	Schrijf het alstublieft.
How are you?	Hoe gaat het met (u/jou)?
I'm fine, thanks.	Goed, bedankt.
What's your name?	Hoe heet u? (polite) Hoe heet je? (informal)
My name is...	Ik heet...
Where are you from?	Waar komt u vandaan? (polite) Waar kom je vandaan? (informal)

I'm from...	Ik kom uit...
Do you have (a)...?	Heeft u (een)...?
How much is it?	Hoeveel is het?
Help!	Help!

Practical Question Words

Who?	Wie?
What?	Wat?
When?	Wanneer?
Where?	Waar?
How?	Hoe?

Accommodation

camping ground	camping
guesthouse	pension
hotel	hotel
youth hostel	jeugdherberg

Do you have any rooms available?	Heeft u kamers vrij?
How much is it per night/ per person?	Hoeveel is het per nacht/ per persoon?
Is breakfast included?	Is het ontbijt inbegrepen?
May I see the room?	Mag ik de kamer zien?

Getting Around

Where is the...?	Waar is...?
bus stop	de bushalte
metro station	het metrostation
train station	het treinstation
tram stop	de tramhalte

What time does the... leave?	Hoe laat vertrekt de...?
What time does the... arrive?	Hoe laat komt de... aan?
bus	bus
train	trein
tram	tram

What street/ road is this?	Welke straat/ weg is dit?

How do I get to...?	Hoe kom ik bij...?
(Go) straight ahead.	(Ga) rechtdoor.
left/right	links/rechts

Are you free? (taxi)	Bent u vrij?
Please put the meter on.	Gebruik de meter alstublieft.
How much is it to ...?	Hoeveel kost het naar ...?
Please take me to (this address).	Breng mij alstublieft naar (dit address).

Around Town

Where is a/the...?	Waar is...?
public toilet	een openbaar toilet
post office	het postkantoor
tourist office	de VVV

Days & Time

Monday	Maandag
Tuesday	Dinsdag
Wednesday	Woensdag
Thursday	Donderdag
Friday	Vrijdag
Saturday	Zaterdag
Sunday	Zondag

What time is it?	Hoe laat is het?
When?	Wanneer?
today	vandaag
yesterday	gisteren
tomorrow	morgen

Numbers

0	nul
1	één
2	twee
3	drie
4	vier
5	vijf
6	zes
7	zeven
8	acht
9	negen

10	tien	1000	duizend
11	elf	one million	miljoen
12	twaalf		
13	dertien		

Emergencies

14 viertien	It's an emergency! Dit is een noodgeval!
15 vijftien	Could you please Kunt u me/ons
16 zestien	help me/us? alstublieft helpen?
17 zeventien	Call the police/ Haal de politie/
18 achttien	a doctor/ een dokter/
19 negentien	an ambulance! een ziekenwagen!
20 twintig	Where's the Waar is het
100 honderd	police station? politiebureau?

Index

SHOPPING

SIGHTS

SLEEPING